Strained Silicon:
A Platform for Next-Generation Optical Devices

Salman Kk

Copyright © [2023]
Author: Salman Kk
Title: Strained Silicon:
A Platform for Next-Generation Optical Devices

All rights reserved. No part of this book may be reproduced or transmitted in any form or by any means, electronic or mechanical, including photocopying, recording, or by any information storage and retrieval system, without permission in writing from the author.

This book is a product of [**Publisher's Salman Kk**]

ISBN:

Contents

1 **INTRODUCTION**   1
   1.1 Electro-optic modulation in silicon   6
      1.1.1 Plasma dispersion effect   7
      1.1.2 Thermo-optic effect   9
      1.1.3 Electro-optic effects   10
   1.2 Structures for electro-optic modulation   11
      1.2.1 Mach-Zehnder interferometers   12
      1.2.2 Ring resonators   14
   1.3 Strained silicon for electro-optic modulation   15
   1.4 Other effects of strain in silicon   19
      1.4.1 Theory of elasticity   19
      1.4.2 Photoelastic effect   22
   1.5 Objectives and outline for this   22

2 **CARRIER EFFECTS AND THEIR INFLUENCE ON THE ELECTRO-OPTIC MEASUREMENTS IN STRAINED SI**   25
   2.1 Fabricated structures   27
   2.2 Experimental setup   28
   2.3 Electro-optical characterization   28
   2.4 Soaking experiments   31
   2.5 Influence of stress magnitude and stress type   34
   2.6 Effect of a thermal annealing   36
   2.7 Raman measurements   38
   2.8 Second harmonic generation experiments   42
      2.8.1 Experimental setup   43
      2.8.2 Theoretical description   44
      2.8.3 Design of the strained silicon waveguides   46
      2.8.4 Experimental results   51

3	EXPLOITATION OF THE OBSERVED FEATURES: AN ELECTRO-OPTIC MEMORY	55
3.1	Non-volatile memory effect in silicon.	56
3.2	A non-volatile photonic memory based on a SAHAS configuration	58
3.2.1	Design of the charge trapping structure	59
3.2.2	Non-volatile photonic device	65
4	TOWARDS POCKELS EFFECT IN STRAINED SILICON	69
4.1	Theoretical models on Pockels effect in strained Silicon	70
4.1.1	Deformation potentials	75
	Second-order susceptibility tensor based on perturbation theory	76
	The unstrained silicon unit cell	79
	Strained silicon and deformation potentials	81
4.1.2	Bond orbital model	84
4.2	Enhancing Pockels effect in strained silicon waveguides	89
4.2.1	The index ellipsoid in strained silicon waveguides	89
4.2.2	The effect of a p-i-n junction	97
4.2.3	The effect of an asymmetric cladding	100
4.3	A $Si_{1-x}Ge_x$ slot approach for the mid-IR range	102
4.3.1	The Ge-SiGe-Si-Ge slot structure	103
	Strain applied to the silicon layer	104
	Electric field strength inside the strained silicon layer	105
4.3.2	The strain induced effective index change	106
5	CONCLUSIONS	110
5.1	Conclusions and future work	110

1
Introduction

THE ROOTS OF Photonics can be traced back to 1962, when the semiconductor laser diode was demonstrated for the first time by the research groups at General Electric and IBM in US[42,47,82,93]. This major discovery was followed, a few years later, by the realisation of low-loss optical fibers capable of transmitting information over long distances[58] which led, in

1988, to the first transatlantic fiber optic cable connecting the US and Europe.

Simultaneously, another field was rapidly and powerfully emerging since 1947, when the first transistor was discovered at Bell Labs. The field of electronics, fueled by silicon as a cornerstone in its fast pace progress, conquered and revolutionised every aspect of our lifestyle. Since then, it has become fundamental in areas as diverse as information, telecommunications, environmental and green technologies, sensing or biomedicine. Such impressive growth was enabled by several key aspects of silicon. First, its extremely low cost compared to other materials, being one of the most abundant element on Earth. Secondly, the landing of the integrated circuits (IC) in 1958, which made possible the large-scale process manufacturing needed for the mass-production of electronic circuits. Since then, not only the price of the silicon chip has been constantly falling, but also the integration capabilities have sustainedly followed the well known Moore's law, doubling the number of transistors per chip every two years, as shown in Fig. 1.1.

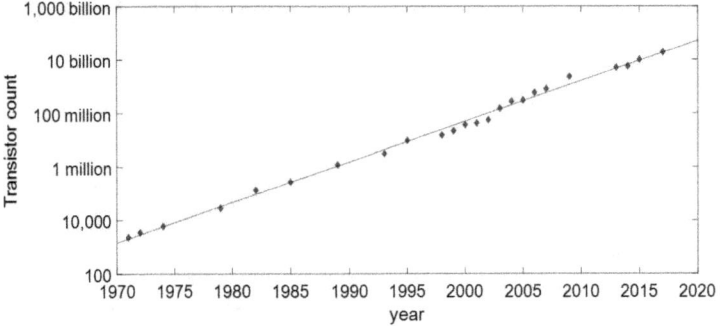

Figure 1.1: Moore's law. Moore's law was the prediction stated by Gordon Moore that the number of transistor per integrated circuit would double every two years. The raw data has been taken from "Our world in data"[102]

Electronics and photonics started to merge in communication systems, when the electrical cables started to be replaced by their optical counterparts in long-distance applications due to their lower signal to noise ratio and increased transmission capabilities. Moreover, with the internet traffic growing 40 %-60% per year[41] and demands continuously increasing, optical cables started to replace wires for shorter and shorter interconnect lengths[73]. In fact, the future goal would be to bring the fiber all the way to the processor[104] and even reach on-chip combined integration of photonic and electronic circuits to take advantage of the strengths of both technologies. Nowadays, information bit rates reach the Tbit/s on the long-distance networks but slow down when passing to the metropolitan-area. In late 2000's optical connectors to link computers up to 300 meters apart started to be commercially available with data rate transmissions of 10 Gb/s. Moreover, optical interconnections are currently being employed in rack-to-rack links among servers in data centers to solve speed bottlenecks. In addition, copper connections inside microprocessors suffer from parasitic resistance, capacitance and inductance, which limit the rate at which they can process information. Those parasitic factors depend on the wire geometry and specially on its length, creating a bottleneck at high frequencies that could be overcome by optically managing that information. Figure 1.2 shows an overview of the future of optical interconnects.

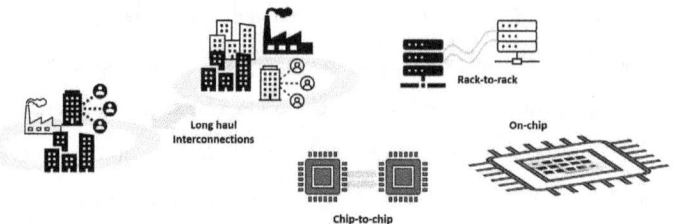

Figure 1.2: Optical interconnections. From long haul information transmission to on-chip optical processing of data.

In addition, although Moore's law has been sustained until today (see Fig. 1.1), limitations in the packing transistor density coming from the leakage currents as well as the RC delay of metal interconnections at such small dimensions are increasing challenges in the microelectronic picture. Moreover, some scientists have even predicted a quantum limit to the Moore's law[91]. Under this framework, silicon photonics comes as a powerful solution for overcoming the electronic bottlenecks at different levels, from the amplification stages in long distance data transmission to even at on-chip scale.

The pioneering works of Soref and Petermann in late 1980s and early 1990s[108,113–115] laid the groundwork of this field and developed the active and passive elements that would become the building blocks of this technology, such as waveguides or electro-optic switchers. Over the past two decades, the field of silicon photonics rapidly expanded and, with it, the diversity of integrated applications ranging from directional couplers[122], multiplexers and de-multiplexers[121], splitters[27,61], electro-optical memories[111] and even efficient light emission[33].

The low-loss window of silicon, extending from 1.1 μm to nearly 7 μm[55], together with its high crystal quality and the strong index contrast between silicon (n=3.47) and silica (n=1.44) offer the possibility of scaling integrated components up to the nanometer level, which is a key requirement for the integration with the electronic industry.

However, important challenges have still to be tackled before reaching mass-market production of photonic integrated circuits (PICs). For instance, the conversion of a high-speed electrical signal into optical digital data is a critical function for modern communication technology, yet, the absence of Pockels effect in silicon inhibits the progress of this technology in such a critical function. The main approach to overcome these limitations has relayed on the plasma dispersion effect, which is currently the most effective mechanism for changing the silicon refractive index at a fast rate[95]. However, a trade off between low driving voltages, high bandwidth and low losses is usually given due to the optical absorption inherent to the plasma dispersion effect. Therefore, different approaches are being followed for trying to have access to high speed electro-optical modulation in the silicon platform. The integration of ferroelectric materials with high Pockels coefficients, such as $LiNbO_3$[94] or $BaTiO_3$[20,127], is currently one of the main approaches. The use of nonlinear polymers with a high second-order nonlinearity has also been proposed[80]. However, the habilitation of Pockels effect in strained silicon via symmetry breaking, as proposed by Jacobsen et al.[53] in 2006, opened the door to a new route for a CMOS compatible integration of fast and low loss electro-optic modulators at minimum complexity and cost. This is the main line of this , to progress in the implementation of efficient Pockels effect in the strained silicon platform. In this section, the methods for realising electro-optic modulation in silicon are reviewed together with a detailed overview of the state-of-the-art on the strained silicon field. At the end, the objectives and outline of this are summarized.

1.1 ELECTRO-OPTIC MODULATION IN SILICON

Electro-optic modulation is the process of varying any of the characteristics of an optical signal by means of an electrically triggered mechanism. The modulating signal causes a direct change in optical intensity via absorption or in its optical phase by changing the refractive index of the material. The concept is schematically illustrated in Fig. 1.3.

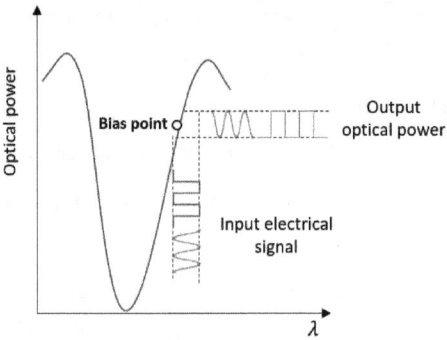

Figure 1.3: Electro-optic modulation. Analog (green) and digital (red) amplitude modulation.

When the phase or intensity of the optical beam is changed in a gradual manner by using a continuous electrical signal, it is referred as *analog* modulation (represented in green in Fig. 1.3). On the other hand, *digital* modulation is achieved (represented in red in Fig. 1.3) when the modulating signal takes the form of a sequence of discrete values, normally two, which are referred as '0's and '1's. Finally, the modulation can be achieved by means of different mechanisms, which will regulate features as important as the modulation efficiency or the modulation speed. Following subsections are dedicated to detail the main physical mechanisms used for modulation in silicon.

1.1.1 PLASMA DISPERSION EFFECT

The plasma dispersion effect is related to the concentration of carriers in a semiconductor and changes both the real and imaginary parts of the refractive index[95]. This effect was firstly described by the Drude-Lorenz model, which relate the electron (N_e) and hole (N_h) concentrations to the absorption and refractive index change in the material:

$$\Delta n = \frac{-e^2 \lambda_0^2}{8\pi^2 c^2 \varepsilon_0 n} \left(\frac{\Delta N_e}{m_{ce}^*} + \frac{\Delta N_h}{m_{ch}^*} \right)$$
$$\Delta \alpha = \frac{e^2 \lambda_0^2}{4\pi^2 c^2 \varepsilon_0 n} \left(\frac{\Delta N_e}{\mu_e (m_{ce}^*)^2} + \frac{\Delta N_h}{\mu_h (m_{ch}^*)^2} \right) \quad (1.1)$$

where e is the electronic charge, λ_0 is the working wavelength, c the velocity of light, m_{ce}^* and $m_c h^*$ are the effective electron and hole masses, ε_0 the vacuum permittivity, n the refractive index of unperturbed silicon, μ_e and μ_h the mobilities of electrons and holes and ΔN_e and ΔN_h the variation of carrier concentrations of electrons and holes.

Soref and Bennett[11] experimentally studied the above relations in silicon, focusing on the telecom wavelengths of 1.3 μm and 1.55 μm. Although the results agreed to a significant extent with the Drude equations, they encountered some deviations from the theory, especially for the hole concentration. They summarized their experimental findings through an empirical relation, which is nowadays almost universally used. For λ_0=1.55 μm is written as:

$$\Delta n = \Delta n_e + \delta n_h = -[8.8 \cdot 10^{-22} \Delta N_e + 8.5 \cdot 10^{-18} (\Delta N_h)^{0.8}]$$
$$\Delta \alpha = \Delta \alpha_e + \Delta \alpha_h = 8.5 \cdot 10^{-18} \Delta N_e + 6.0 \cdot 10^{-18} \Delta N_h \quad (1.2)$$

where δn_e, δn_h are the change in refractive index due to the concentration of electrons and holes and $\Delta \alpha_e$, $\Delta \alpha_h$ are the change in absorption coefficients for electrons and holes.

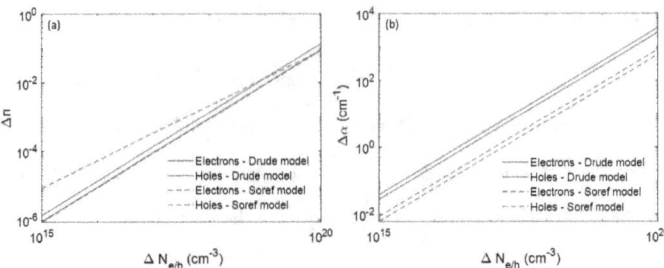

Figure 1.4: Comparison of Drude and Soref models. Comparison of the Drude and Soref predictions for (a) the refractive index and (b) the absorption coefficient for carrier concentrations in the range 10^{15} cm^{-3} to 10^{20} cm^{-3}.

Figure 1.4 shows the comparison of the theoretical prediction obtained from the Drude model and that obtained with the empirical equations. In fact, the linear dependency for the index change of electrons agree in both models, however, holes show a smaller slope in the Soref case. In addition, absorption is slightly overestimated for both, electrons and holes, in the Drude's model.

In addition, the plasma dispersion effect can be quantified based on the above equations. Refractive index variations of around 10^{-3} are achievable with carrier concentrations about 10^{18} cm^{-3}, although absorption losses of 10 cm^{-1} are associated to this change. Based on these values and due to its high-speed modulation, plasma dispersion effect is considered the most efficient way of modulation up to date[95].The first plasma dispersion silicon modulator was realised in 2004 by re-using the concept of the metal-oxide-silicon capacitor[70]. This type of structures were improved in the following years and they are generally based on changing the mode effective index thanks to the carrier accumulation next to the oxide gate. Modulation up to 10 Gbit/s[67] was demonstrated in a Mach-Zehnder interferometer (MZI) based on accumulation of free carriers.

On the other hand, devices based on carrier injection usually consist on a p-i-n junction where a minority carrier flows through the intrinsic region overlapping the guided mode. These structures show both, electro-refraction and electro-absorption due to the high amount of injected carriers. The high modulation efficiency leads to short modulation lengths with the counterpart of high insertion losses and power consumption. In addition, speeds are limited to around 1 Gbit/s due to the slow carrier generation/recombination processes. Despite the aforementioned, speeds up to 18 Gbit/s have been demonstrated using a pre-amplification phase in a silicon ring resonator[76].

Finally, depletion based modulators work by changing the width of the depletion region of a p-n junction. This effect is intrinsically faster because no generation/recombination processes are involved, however, they show inferior modulation efficiency due to the lower carrier concentrations. Modulation up to 40 Gbit/s has been demonstrated in various devices with lengths ranging between 1 mm to 3.5 mm[66,119].

1.1.2 Thermo-optic effect

Alternatively, the modulation can be carried out through thermo-optic effect, which, owing the large thermo-optic coefficient os silicon:

$$\frac{\Delta n}{\Delta T} = 1.86 \cdot 10^{-4} K^{-1} \qquad (1.3)$$

allows for a high modulation efficiency. A refractive index change of $\sim 10^{-3}$ can be achieved with a temperature difference of only 5ºC[95]. Experimental demonstrations have proven that a phase shift of π can be achieved with a length of 500 μm with an applied power to the metal heater of $\sim$10mW[26]. The major counterpart of this effect relays in its rather low speed in the microsecond range. Therefore, thermo-optic effect is the first option whenever the speed is not critical.

1.1.3 ELECTRO-OPTIC EFFECTS

Electro-optic effects appear when a static or low-frequency electric field is applied to a material and produce a bond charge redistribution [129] leading to a change in the polarization and, hence, in the material refractive index. They are related to the second $\chi^{(2)}{}_{ijk}$ and third order $\chi^{(3)}{}_{ijkl}$ susceptibility tensors and are also called linear and quadratic electro-optic effects due to their dependency on the applied electric field:

$$P_i^{(2)} = 2\epsilon_0 \sum_{jk} \chi^{(2)}{}_{ijk}(\omega = \omega + 0) E_j(\omega) E_k(0) \tag{1.4}$$

$$P_i^{(3)} = 3\epsilon_0 \sum_{jkl} \chi^{(3)}{}_{ijkl}(\omega = \omega + 0 + 0) E_j(\omega) E_k(0) E_l(0) \tag{1.5}$$

where $P_i^{(n)}$ is the i-th component of the n-th order material polarization, ϵ_0 is the vacuum dielectric permittivity and E_j, E_k, E_l are the cartesian components of the electric field.

In addition, they are also referred as Pockels and Kerr effect, respectively and, whenever both are present in the material, the first dominates over the second. However, in the case of silicon, the Pockels effect vanishes due to the inversion symmetry of its lattice. Therefore, efficient modulation via Pockels effect has been only demonstrated to date by integrating other materials such as $LiNbO_3$ [56], which is also used in commercial devices. Kerr effect has also been explored [31]. Moreover, third-order nonlinearities in silicon have also been exploited through electric field-induced second harmonic-generation (EFISH), where a static electric field couples with the $\chi^{(3)}$ of silicon to give rise to an effective second order susceptibility of $\chi^{(2)}_{EFISH} = 3\chi^{(3)}E(0)$. In this way, high frequency modulation has been demonstrated through a periodically varying p-i-n junction[120], estimating an electric field induced $\chi^{(2)}_{EFISH}$ of ~40 pm/V. Following a similar approach, high frequency modulation was proposed by using layers of AlO_2 and SiN to achieve charges of opposite signs at the interfaces and, hence, inducing a $\chi^{(2)}_{EFISH}$[68] in those layers.

Finally, the possibility of exploiting Pockels effect in silicon via symmetry breaking due to an applied strain would enable efficient ultrahigh-speed modulation without penalizing losses and would represent a milestone in silicon photonics. Strained silicon was proposed around 15 years ago to achieve this goal via symmetry breaking. It is the main line of this and will be extensively explained in Section 1.3.

1.2 STRUCTURES FOR ELECTRO-OPTIC MODULATION

The physical mechanisms for electro-optic modulation in silicon have been presented in the previous section. Such mechanisms change the real and/or the imaginary part of the material refractive index. The change in the imaginary part directly changes the intensity of the optical signal, however, a change in the real part acts only by changing its phase. The phase shift has to be then translated to intensity variation by integrating the phase shifter structure into an intensity modulator, commonly a Mach-Zehnder interferometer (MZI) or a ring resonator. The operation principles of such devices are detailed in the following sections.

1.2.1 Mach-Zehnder interferometers

Mach-Zehnder interferometers work by splitting the input light in two beams. Either a Y-junction or a MMI is ussually in charge of this task. After that, each of the beams travels down two paths that induce a phase difference between both beams. The phase difference can be implemented by inducing a refractive index change through any of the mechanisms described in Secs. 1.1.1-1.1.3. The light is then recombined, producing an interference and, thus, generating an output signal modulated in amplitude. The device is schematically depicted in Fig. 1.5, where the modulating mechanism is electrically triggered by applying a voltage difference between two electrodes.

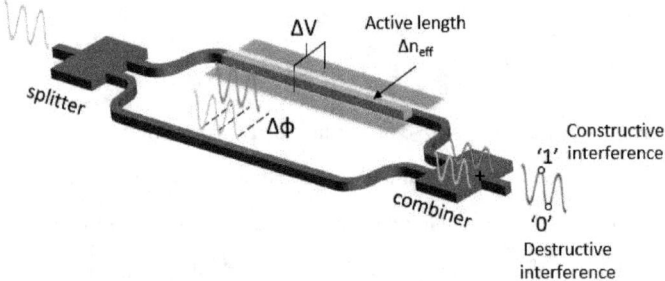

Figure 1.5: Scheme of a Mach-Zehnder interferometer.

Therefore, after passing through both arms of the MZI, each of the beams has a phase ϕ_1 and ϕ_2 and a shift between them of $\Delta\phi = \phi_2 - \phi_1$, which can be expressed as

$$\Delta\phi = \frac{2\pi}{\lambda}\Delta n_{eff} L_{active} \qquad (1.6)$$

where L_{active} is the active length of the device and Δn_{eff} the induced effective index change. This equation is valid for symmetric MZIs. On the other hand, if propagation losses are neglected, the power of the output signal P_{out} can be calculated as

$$\frac{P_{out}}{P_{in}} = cos^2(\Delta\phi/2) \qquad (1.7)$$

where P_{in} is the input power. Depending on the induced phase mismatch, therefore, it is possible to control the spectral response of the device, i.e. to control where, in the spectral domain, a constructive or a destructive interference is achieved when combining both signals. The concept is depicted in Fig. 1.6.

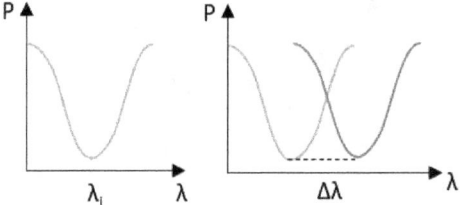

Figure 1.6: Spectral shift due to the modulation in a MZI.

In addition, if the spectral shift $\Delta\lambda$ is known from experimental measurements, it is possible to calculate the effective index change that produced such spectral shift:

$$\Delta n_{eff} = \frac{\Delta\lambda}{\lambda} n_g \frac{\Delta L}{L_{active}} \qquad (1.8)$$

where n_g is the group index, λ the working wavelength and ΔL is the length difference between both arms of the MZI, if present.

1.2.2 RING RESONATORS

Figure 1.7 shows a scheme of a ring resonator, which consists on a bus straight waveguide placed at a distance d of a ring with a radius R. The distance d is also called the *coupling distance* because it determines the amount of light coupled to the ring waveguide.

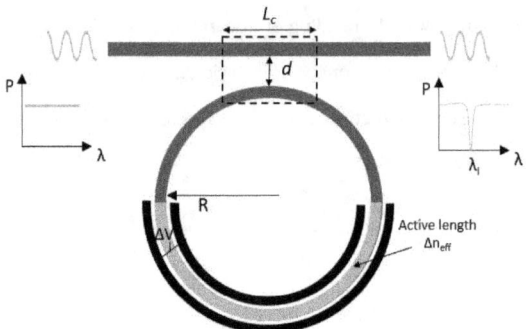

Figure 1.7: Scheme of a ring resonator.

The input light is injected to the device through the input port and, whenever its wavelength coincides with the propagation length of the resonator, a minimum in the output power is achieved. This requirement is mathematically expressed as

$$n_{eff} L_{ring} = N \lambda_i \tag{1.9}$$

where n_{eff} is the effective refractive index, $L_{ring}=2\pi R$ the total length of the ring, N is an integer and λ_i with i=1,2... is each of the wavelengths that fulfills the condition.

Therefore, the output optical power is minimum at the resonance wavelength λ_i. The amount of output power at such wavelength will depend on the coupling conditions and will only be null when the device is working at critical coupling, i.e. when the coupled power is the same as the power lost in the ring. The coupling conditions can be managed through designing the coupling distance and the coupling length L_c.

Similar to the case of the MZI, a spectral shift of the resonance will occur if a refractive index change is induced in the structure, as depicted in Fig. 1.8

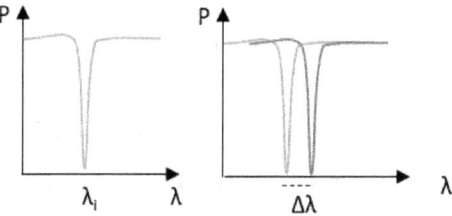

Figure 1.8: Spectral shift due to the modulation in a ring resonator.

The relationship between the obtained spectral shift and the effective index change induced in the optical mode can be written as

$$\Delta n_{eff} = \frac{\Delta \lambda}{\lambda} n_g \frac{L_{ring}}{L_{active}} \qquad (1.10)$$

1.3 STRAINED SILICON FOR ELECTRO-OPTIC MODULATION

Despite the enormous growth of silicon photonics in the last decades, the lack of second-order nonlinearities poses a major challenge in the progress of this technology, being forced to either rely in less efficient mechanisms to implement high frequency switching or having to integrate other materials such as LiNbO3 [56] or BTO [1] and, hence, losing CMOS compatibility.

A new method for enabling Pockels effect in silicon was published for the first time by Jacobsen et al. [54] in 2006. The inversion symmetry of the silicon lattice was broken by means of a stressor cover layer, giving rise to an induced non-linear optic coefficient of $\chi^{(2)}$ ~15 pm/V and paving the way for a new class of integrated silicon devices fully compatible with the microelectronic industry. The possibility of achieving quasi-phase matching (QPM) by means of alternating stress fields along a silicon waveguide was theorized to further enhance the non-linear effect [48].

In 2011, the first fully integrated strained Mach Zehnder interferometer was published by Chmielak et al. [24] with an associated $\chi^{(2)}$ as large as 122 pm/V which was positively correlated with the waveguide strain measured using micro-Raman mappings [13], hence, strongly supporting the evidence of a strain induced effect. This work was the seed for their next publication, where the same authors reached a value of $\chi^{(2)}$=190 pm/V by engineering the waveguide geometry [23]. A linear relationship between the effective refractive index and the applied voltage was demonstrated in the aforementioned works, thus, identifying Pockels effect as the origin of the measured $\chi^{(2)}$. Following studies reached even larger nonlinear values [29,75], achieving a record $\chi^{(2)}$ of 360 pm/V [29] in 2014, which is comparable to that of commercially available modulators.

However, ambiguous results started to arise in experimental measurements. In 2015, Azadeh et. al. [7] revealed the key role played by free and trapped carriers in the obtained results of strained silicon MZIs. The role of trap centers at the interface of silicon and silicon nitride, inducing the characteristic hysteretic effect observed in strained silicon devices was also evidenced[85]. Furthermore, it was shown that the linear relation between effetive index change and applied voltage could be inverted by depositing a cover layer with trapped charges of the opposite sign[109]. In addition, homodyne detection technique was used to monitor the electro-optic response of strained silicon ring resonators, showing anomalous responses incompatible with Pockels effect which could be accounted based only on free-carrier effects[14]. A maximum value of strain induced $\chi^{(2)}$ of 8 pm/V was set based on these findings.

Moreover, second-harmonic generation (SHG) experiments also extracted much lower $\chi^{(2)}$ coefficients, in the order of several or tens pm/V[21,107] and it was later theorized that the origin of those results could be not in the silicon itself but rather in the silicon nitride layer[59] or in a electric-field induced effect (EFISH) created due to the trapped charges in the cover layer[19].

Regarding the theoretical perspective, several models relying in experimentally determined coefficients were published[75,92] while the existence of a discrepancy between theoretical and experimental was highlighted by different studies[49]. A theoretical model developed back in 1989 based on deformation potentials[39] and contrasted later with Raman measurements[51] predicted much lower values of $\chi^{(2)}$. A more recent work based on the bond orbital model also pointed to the same direction, reporting theoretical values in the order of several pm/V[30]. The coefficients of this model were then adjusted to experimental data to fit real device performance, throwing theoretical results compatible with experimental responses of strained MZIs[28].

All the aforementioned results made clear that the strain induced $\chi^{(2)}$ could not be much larger than a few pm/V. In addition, fast linear electro-optic effect has been recently demonstrated in a strained silicon MZI[12]. Modulation was shown up to 10 GHz, which is above the characteristic frequencies of plasma dispersion effect and, therefore, makes possible to identify Pockels effect as the underlying mechanism. The observed response was coherent with the theoretical model proposed previously by Damas et al.[30] and fitted to experimental values[28], demonstrating a $\chi^{(2)}$ value of 1.8 pm/V. An overview of the $\chi^{(2)}$ experimental values reported to date in strained silicon devices is detailed in Table 1.1.

Year	$\chi^{(2)}(pm/V)$	Ref.
2006	15	[54]
2011	122	[24]
2013	190	[23]
2014	360	[29]
2015	<8	[14]
2018	1.8	[12]

Table 1.1: Experimental values of $\chi^{(2)}$. Overview of the experimental $\chi^{(2)}$ coefficients reported to date.

It is clear, therefore, that the low $\chi^{(2)}$ coefficients exhibited by strained silicon must be strongly enhanced before reaching practical values for efficient modulation, which has been the main goal of this . With this aim, the masking effect of trapped and free carriers were studied in a first work[85]. Then, a p-i-n junction was proposed to eliminate the adverse influence of free and trapped carriers in the electro-optic response of strained silicon devices. Moreover, using an asymmetric stress cladding (that is, each half of the cladding layer having opposite intrinsic stress) an enhancement factor of 200 in the strain induced effective index change was achieved[86] with respect to the conventional silicon-silicon nitride covered waveguide used in previous studies. In addition, the possibility of using germanium to induce more intense strains in silicon has also been proposed together with a slot configuration to further enhance the nonlinearities[87], reaching an enhancement factor of more than three orders of magnitude.

1.4 OTHER EFFECTS OF STRAIN IN SILICON

The use of strain may enable efficient modulation in silicon, however, other properties of the material can be also affected when applying strain. In this section we will first detail the basic principles of elasticity followed by a brief explanation of the photoelastic effect. This effect has been considered in the design and analysis of second harmonic generation experiments in Sec. 2.8.

1.4.1 THEORY OF ELASTICITY

When a material suffers a deformation, any point of the material characterized by a vector position $\vec{r}$ will be displaced to a new location $\vec{r}'$. The total displacement thus can be written as

$$\vec{u} = \vec{r}' - \vec{r} \qquad (1.11)$$

Considering Eq. 1.11, it is possible to define the symmetric strain tensor ε that describes such deformation:

$$\varepsilon_{ij} = \frac{1}{2}\left(\frac{\partial u_i}{\partial x_j} + \frac{\partial u_j}{\partial x_i}\right) \qquad (1.12)$$

where i,j are x,y,z. The relationship between how a material is deformed by an applied stress is dictated by the generalized Hooke's law, which relates the strain ε and stress σ tensors:

$$\varepsilon = C\sigma$$
$$\sigma = S\varepsilon \qquad (1.13)$$

where C and S are the fourth-rank tensors called compliance and stiffness tensors. For anisotropic materials, their 81 elements are in general independent and non null, however, crystal symmetries usually reduce the number of independent coefficients. In the case of silicon and germanium, which are materials with inversion symmetry, there are only three independent values and the stiffness matrix takes the following form:

$$s_{pq} = \begin{bmatrix} s_{11} & s_{12} & s_{12} & 0 & 0 & 0 \\ s_{12} & s_{11} & s_{12} & 0 & 0 & 0 \\ s_{12} & s_{12} & s_{11} & 0 & 0 & 0 \\ 0 & 0 & 0 & s_{44} & 0 & 0 \\ 0 & 0 & 0 & 0 & s_{44} & 0 \\ 0 & 0 & 0 & 0 & 0 & s_{44} \end{bmatrix} \qquad (1.14)$$

where contracted notation has been used and the indexes p,q can take therefore values from 1 to 6. The elements s_{pq} are listed in Table 1.2 for silicon and germanium.

	s_{11}	s_{12}	s_{44}
	($cm^2/10^{12}$ dyn)		
Si	0.768	-0.214	1.26
Ge	0.964	-0.260	1.49
SiO$_2$	1.304	-0.2425	3.09
SiN	0.392	-0.0916	0.964

Table 1.2: The stiffness coefficients for silicon and germanium taken from [125] and for SiN and SiO$_2$ taken from [130] and [32], respectively.

For isotropic materials such as silicon nitride or silicon oxide in their amorphous phases, the tensors C and S take a similar form as in Eq. 1.14 but their s_{pq} coefficients show no dependence with crystal orientation. The case is different for silicon and germanium. In fact, the values shown in Table 1.2 are those considering the coordinate system aligned with the [100],[010],[001] crystal directions.

For an arbitrary rotation from crystal axes x_i to a new system with axes x'_i being i=1,2,3, we can relate:

$$x'_i = l_i x_1 + m_i x_2 + n_i x_3 \qquad (1.15)$$

where l, m, n are the direction cosines of the transformation. Considering Eq. 1.15, it is possible to calculate the stiffness coefficients in the new system as [125]

$$s'_{ii} = s_{11} + s_c(l_i^4 + m_i^4 + n_i^4 - 1) \text{ with } i = 1,2,3$$

$$s'_{ij} = s_{12} + s_c(l_i^2 l_j^2 + m_i^2 m_j^2 + n_i^2 n_j^2) \text{ with } ij = 13, 12, 23$$

$$s'_{rq} = s'_{ijkp} = 4s_c(l_i l_j l_k l_p + m_i m_j m_k m_p + n_i n_j n_k n_p) \text{ with } rq = 46, 45, 56$$

$$s'_{rq} = s'_{ijkp} = 2s_c(l_i l_j l_k l_p + m_i m_j m_k m_p + n_i n_j n_k n_p) \text{ with } rq = 14, 36, 25, 24, 26, 34, 16, 35$$

$$s'_{rq} = s'_{ijkp} = s_{44} + 4s_c(l_i l_j l_k l_p + m_i m_j m_k m_p + n_i n_j n_k n_p) \text{ with } rq = 44, 55, 66$$

$$(1.16)$$

where contracted notation has been used and the subscripts rq represent two subscrips

$$1 \to 11, 2 \to 22, 3 \to 33, 4 \to 23, 5 \to 13, 6 \to 12 \qquad (1.17)$$

During this , we will usually deal with rotations in the (100)-plane. Values from Eq. 1.16 will be used unless stated otherwise. In addition, whenever a $Si_{1-x}Ge_x$ alloy will be used, it will be supposed that the values of the coefficients will vary linearly with Ge concentration, thus, they will be determined by interpolating from pure Si and Ge values.

1.4.2 PHOTOELASTIC EFFECT

The photoelastic effect describes the changes in the optical properties of a material that undergoes a mechanical deformation. Considering a diamond structure such as that of silicon, when a stress is applied, the components of the refractive index can be rewritten as [52]

$$\begin{bmatrix} n_{xx} \\ n_{yy} \\ n_{zz} \\ n_{yz} \\ n_{xz} \\ n_{xy} \end{bmatrix} = \begin{bmatrix} n_0 \\ n_0 \\ n_0 \\ n_0 \\ n_0 \\ n_0 \end{bmatrix} - 0.5 n_0^3 \begin{bmatrix} p_{11} & p_{12} & p_{12} & 0 & 0 & 0 \\ p_{12} & p_{11} & p_{12} & 0 & 0 & 0 \\ p_{12} & p_{12} & p_{11} & 0 & 0 & 0 \\ 0 & 0 & 0 & p_{44} & 0 & 0 \\ 0 & 0 & 0 & 0 & p_{44} & 0 \\ 0 & 0 & 0 & 0 & 0 & p_{44} \end{bmatrix} \cdot \begin{bmatrix} \varepsilon_{xx} \\ \varepsilon_{yy} \\ \varepsilon_{zz} \\ \varepsilon_{yz} \\ \varepsilon_{xz} \\ \varepsilon_{xy} \end{bmatrix} \quad (1.18)$$

where n_0 is the refractive index of the unstrained material and p_{pq} are the photoelastic coefficients which take the values p_{11}=-0.0997, p_{12}=-0.0107 and $p_{44} = (p_{11} - p_{12})/2$=-0.051 in silicon [52].

1.5 OBJECTIVES AND OUTLINE FOR THIS

Despite the enormous advance of silicon photonics over the last decade, the integration of some of the main building blocks in the standard CMOS silicon process is still limited. One of such building blocks is the electro-optic modulator, in charge of the conversion of high-speed electrical signal into optical data. The most efficient way of achieving such functionality in silicon up to date is by using the plasma dispersion effect. Nevertheless, this mechanism shows an intrinsic trade-off between improved voltage and bandwidth performance and low losses. In this situation, strained silicon appeared in 2006 as a disruptive solution for enabling ultra-fast efficient modulation in a simple and fully CMOS compatible manner. But despite the stimulating initial results, several issues soon appeared limiting the progress of such technology. Within this context, the work of this has been performed with the aim of facing the emerging challenges and to advance towards enabling Pockels effect in strained silicon.

This introductory Chapter 1 is aimed at giving a general overview of silicon photonics and how strained silicon fits in that p icture. The current physical mechanisms for optical modulation in silicon are also described followed by the state of the art of strained silicon, showing its challenges but also its ground-breaking potential to push forward the progress of photonics. In addition, the basic theory of elasticity and photoelastic effect is also given, as they are concurrent phenomenon affecting the performance of silicon devices whenever a strain is present.

Chapter 2 delves on how carrier effects influence the performance of strained silicon devices and tries to estimate the magnitude of the stress induced $\chi^{(2)}$. With this aim, the chapter is divided in two main sections. First, the electro-optic response of silicon Mach-Zehnder interferometers is studied. The influence of device orientation, a characteristic feature of $\chi^{(2)}$ processes, as well as the impact of stress magnitude and stress type are analyzed by means of silicon nitride layers with different intrinsic stress v alues. An annealing step is performed on the fabricated samples to further evaluate how a change in stress affects the structures and Raman measurements are carried out to clarify the origin of the obtained results. Finally, second harmonic generation experiments are performed in the last section to detect the effective magnitude of $\chi^{(2)}$ present in strained silicon waveguides.

Among the other building blocks lacking in silicon photonics, the non-volatile memory cell is one with a major importance. In Chapter 3, the trapping properties observed in the fabricated devices of Chapter 2 are investigated to achieve an electro-optic memory. In fact, the trapping of carriers in a dielectric material is widely used in microelectronics to implement the memory functionality. A similar approach is followed in this work to enable a fully CMOS compatible electro-optic memory.

In Chapter 4, a step forward is taken for achieving practical values of strain induced Pockels effect. After a brief overview of the main theoretical models linking strain and $\chi^{(2)}$, two approaches to enhance Pockels effect in strained silicon are discussed: a p-i-n juntion and a Si-Ge slot waveguide.

Finally, the conclusions and future work are discussed in Chapter 5.

2

Carrier effects and their influence on the electro-optic measurements in strained Si

IN THE LAST YEARS, discrepancies between theoretical and experimental results in strained silicon devices have made relevant that other effects could also be taking place in the measured responses[106]. The influence of carrier effects have been demonstrated to play a prominent role in the electro-optic response[7,14,15,109] and high frequency measurements have shown a modulation signal vanishing for speeds much faster than the effective carrier lifetime[15]. It has been demonstrated that the free carrier distribution inside the silicon waveguide depends on the fixed charge of the cladding layer[7,109]. Moreover, variations of the carrier distribution can affect the electric field inside the waveguide and, therefore, the modulation induced by the Pockels effect. Therefore, it is necessary to untangle the concurrent mechanisms present in strained silicon devices. The tensor nature of $\chi^{(2)}$ makes second order nonlinear effects dependent on the crystallographic orientation and, within the current picture, this rotational dependency comes as a valuable tool to identify any contribution of Pockels effect. In the same line, second harmonic generation is a sensitive $\chi^{(2)}$ phenomena not affected by free carriers which can be used to detect the presence of a strain induced $\chi^{(2)}$.

This chapter delves on how carrier and interface traps affect the response of strained silicon devices and explores different mechanisms to try to uniquely identify the presence of Pockels effect. In Secs. 2.1 and 2.2 the fabricated structures and the experimental setup are introduced. In Sec. 2.3, the electro-optic characterization of strained MZIs is performed. Their rotational dependency as well as the influence of trapped charges at the silicon-silicon nitride interface is analysed. Moreover, soaking experiments are carried out in Sec. 2.4 and the impact of the stress magnitude and stress type is studied in Sec. 2.5. The influence of an additional annealing step, which changes the intrinsic stress of the silicon nitride, is carried out in the following section 2.6 together with Raman measurements in Sec. 2.7. Finally, in Sec. 2.8, second harmonic generation experiments are performed in strained waveguides to further investigate the existence of non-linearities in this platform.

2.1 Fabricated structures

A set of Mach-Zehnder interferometers were fabricated in a (100) Si wafer placed at varying angles with respect to the crystallographic axis of silicon. More specifically, the Mach-Zehnders were placed at 0º, 30º, 60º and 90º with respect each other, as shown in the sketch of Figure 2.1. The MZIs were designed with a length difference of 180 μm between both arms. The waveguide structure was fabricated using a silicon-on-insulator (SOI) wafer with a silicon height of 220 nm thickness. A full etch depth and a waveguide width of 400 nm was chosen to increase the stress at the walls and to support the TE fundamental mode. Furthermore, the thickness and fabrication process of the PECVD (plasma enhanced chemical vapour deposition) silicon nitride layer was optimized to achieve a tensile stress of 420 GPa with a thickness of 700 nm and deposited on top as a cover layer. Alumnium electrodes were placed on top of the silicon nitride resulting in an active length of 1 mm. A cross-section of the device is depicted in the inset of Fig. 2.1 showing the structure dimensions.

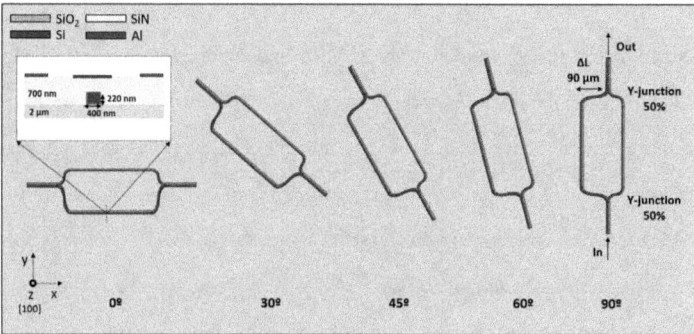

Figure 2.1: Fabricated sample with strained Mach-Zehnder interferometers. Off-scale sketch of the fabricated sample showing the orientation of the strained Mach-Zehnder interferometers together with an inset of the structure cross-section.

2.2 Experimental setup

The experimental setup used during this work is sketched in Fig. 2.2. The source is a continuous-wave laser working in the wavelength band from 1540 nm to 1570 nm and is carried to a polarizer before reaching the coupling stage. The light is then vertically coupled to the test structures by using grating couplers. After passing through the sample, the output light is again collected and finally detected by using a photodetector.

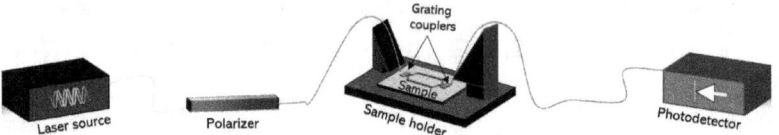

Figure 2.2: Electro-optical characterization setup. Offscale sketch of the setup used for the electro-optic characterization.

2.3 Electro-optical characterization

The electro-optical characterization of the Mach-Zehnder interferometers is shown in Fig. 2.3. As an example, the spectrum of the device rotated 0º is shown in Fig. 2.3(a), while its behavior as a function of the applied voltage is shown in Fig. 2.3 (b) for the resonance centered at $\sim$1550 nm. A complete cycle starting from 0V up to 120 V, going down to -120 V and back to 0V was performed to analyze the observed anomalies. In fact, the resonance taken at 0V is shifted whenever is measured after passing through $\pm$120 V, thus, revealing the presence of hysteresis, a feature certainly not attributable to Pockels effect. Such hysteresis is present in all measured devices as also reflected in Fig. 2.3(c). Maximum effective index changes around $\pm 10^{-4}$ are obtained for all devices and, although there are some differences between the results obtained at different orientations, those differences are in the order of $\sim$0.1-0.2·10^{-4}, which indicates that the observed variations in the effective index change of differently oriented devices are not significant.

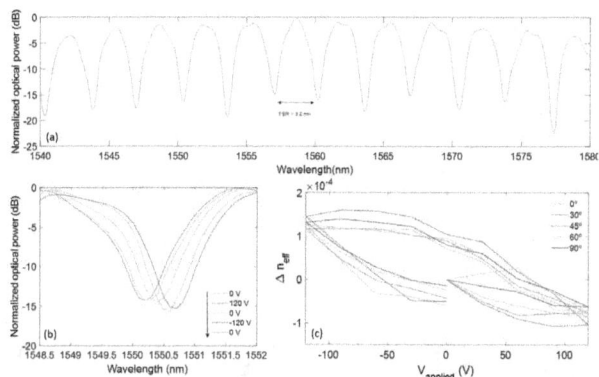

Figure 2.3: Electro-optical characterization of strained Mach-Zehnder interferometers with different orientations. (a) Spectra of the MZI with 0° orientation, (b) resonance shift as a function of the applied voltage for the 0° oriented MZI and (c) effective index change obtained for the fabricated devices with orientation varying from 0° to 90°.

Moreover, in addition to the observed hysteresis, a saturation effect can be noticed for high negative voltages when the index change remains rather constant despite the increase in voltage. Such features are not compatible with the linear relationship expected if Pockels effect was the underlying mechanism and forces us to find other causes for the observed results.

With this aim, simulations have been carried out to analyze the potential impact of the free carrier redistribution inside the silicon waveguide on the measured response. A FEM (finite element method) based software, SILVACO[110], was used to perform the simulations. The results of effective index change as a function of the applied voltage are shown in Fig.

2.4 (a) for different fixed charge concentrations at the silicon-silicon nitride interface. As it was also pointed out by Azadeh et al.[7], a fixed charge stored in the silicon nitride film causes a displacement of the index curve, which may give rise to a linear response in a certain range of applied voltages.

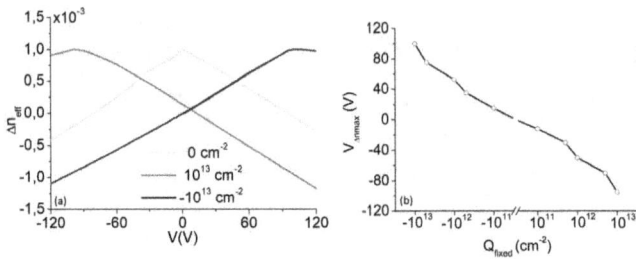

Figure 2.4: Free carrier simulation results. (a) Effective index change obtained by simulations for different fixed charge concentrations and (d) voltage at which the index curve is centered as a function of the fixed charge.

Fig. 2.4(b) shows the voltage at which the index curve is centered depending on the fixed charge. Typical values reported for silicon nitride are on the order of $1\text{-}5 \cdot 10^{12} cm^{-2}$ so that simulations have been carried out in the range $[-10^{13}, 10^{13}]$ cm^{-2} to take into account high densities that could ocurr due to the large applied voltages. In fact, the linear relationship of the experimental response with the applied voltage would be in agreement with simulations in case that the positive fixed charge stored within the silicon nitride was around $10^{13} cm^{-2}$. However, a discrepancy of around one order of magnitude is found between the simulated and the experimental effective refractive index change. While the maximum effective index change given by simulations is in the order of 10^{-3}, the experimental one only reaches 10^{-4}. The origin of this discrepancy is attributed to a charge interchange at the interface between silicon and silicon nitride, which would also explain the presence of the hysteresis and saturation effects.

2.4 Soaking experiments

The trapping properties of silicon nitride films have been extensively studied in the microelectronics industry. The material is known due to its high defect concentration, positive fixed charge and ability to trap carriers from the silicon substrate in MOSFET devices[123,124]. Although charge in the bulk or away from the interface is actually fixed, there is some amount which is nearer to the interface that can be interchanged between silicon and silicon nitride. The amount of fixed charge is usually studied using metal-insulator-semiconductor (MIS) structures. The charge of defects and dangling bonds can be altered at the interface or near the interface by applying a bias, causing the trapping and detrapping of carriers and resulting in a varying fixed charge, Q_{fixed}[10], and hysteresis in the C-V measurement. Furthermore, the creation of new interface traps is well documented due to processes such as bias temperature instability (BTI). When high voltages are applied to the gate, high carrier concentrations are accumulated next to the interface and Si-H, N-H bonds can be broken mediated by a carrier trapping mechanism, giving rise to a great amount of new interface traps[4,63,116]. Both are slow processes involving the release and diffusion of hydrogen at the interface and usually take place in a range from less than seconds to minutes and hours. Since our measurement time is around two minutes for each measured voltage, those processes can be taking place when we perform the hysteresis cycle. In order to further investigate if BTI processes are present in our devices soaking measurements have been carried out. Experiments performed in MIS structures usually consist in a constant gate applied voltage during a large period of time and a relax phase at 0V during a similar range of time. The same procedure has been applied to our devices, maintaining a voltage of -120V during one hour and monitoring the resonance shift of the MZI response. The measured variation of the effective index with time is depicted in Fig. 2.5(a). It can be seen that the index change decays with time at almost half of its initial value. The rate at which traps are being created is usually characterized with a time dependency in the form

$$\Delta N_{it} = At^n \qquad (2.1)$$

where n is typically in the range of 0.2-0.3 for negative BTI (NBTI)[4,63,116]. The effective index variation when the high voltage is applied has been fitted to an analogous time dependency to confirm its presence. The result is depicted in Fig. 2.5(b), showing an almost perfect fit (R^2=0.992) and obtaining a value of n=0.2197 for the exponent, which would agree quite well with the theory of a NBTI process. The behavior of the optical absorption has also been characterized by means of a straight waveguide fabricated in the same sample. An electrode equal to that used on the MZI was located on top of the waveguide and an analogous measurement procedure was carried out. Figure 2.5(a) shows also the evolution of the absorption with time. Absorption values are negative indicating that they are lower compared to that at 0V and increase with time until the voltage of -120 V is no longer applied. This behavior is also in agreement with the creation of new interface traps. The trapping of more carriers gradually increases the silicon nitride fixed charge and consequently the absorption becomes higher with time while the effective index change decays.

In addition, the influence of interface traps on the electro-optic response has been analyzed by means of simulations. A continuous interface trap density distribution in energy is usually found within the silicon band gap. Moreover, the minimum density is generally found

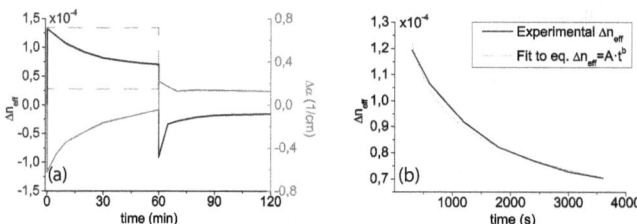

Figure 2.5: Experimental effective index change and absorption time evolution.(a) Time evolution of the absorption and effective index change for the soaking experiments. At the high voltage phase, shown in a dashed square, voltage was kept constant at -120V during the first 60 minutes. The recovery phase at 0V was monitored during the subsequent hour. (b) Effective index fit to the theoretical time dependency of Eq. (2.1) for the high voltage phase.

for stoichiometric or near stoichiometric silicon nitride films [103], however, for samples with a nitride to silicon ratio [N]/[Si] of 1.5, far from the stoichiometric one (1.33), trap density values around $1 \cdot 10^{13} cm^{-2}$ [10] are also measured in MIS structures when high voltages are applied.

Taking that into account, a distribution of traps located at the silicon-silicon nitride interface was added to the simulations, considering an additional fixed charge of $8 \cdot 10^{12} cm^{-2}$ and the interface trap parameters shown in Table 2.1 with the typical capture cross sections reported in the literature [105]. As shown in Fig. 2.6, simulated values very close to those experimentally observed were obtained. Both, the experimental and simulated effective index change (Fig. 2.6(a)) and optical absorption (Fig. 2.6(b)) are in the same order of magnitude. Furthermore, although it was not possible to include the time dependency and so the hysteresis effect is not present in the simulations, the variation with the applied voltage is also in good agreement, thus supporting the influence and presence of interface states at the silicon-silicon nitride interface. Due to the fact that hysteresis has not been included, the only part of the experimental curve that could be simulated is the continuous one from 120V to -120V.

Therefore, in Fig. 2.6, the effective index change and absorption are normalized to the corresponding values at 0V of this part of the hysteresis cycle.

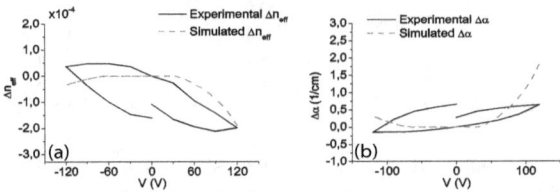

Figure 2.6: Simulation and experimental results comparison. The simulated (a) refractive index change and (b) absorption have been obtained taking into account the interface traps parameters depicted in Table 2.1.

Energy level	Density(cm^{-2})	σ_n (cm^{-2})	σ_p (cm^{-2})
E_{trap}-E_v(eV)	Donor states		
0.6	$6 \cdot 10^{12}$	10^{-18}	10^{-18}
0.4	$7 \cdot 10^{12}$	10^{-13}	10^{-13}
0.2	$8 \cdot 10^{12}$	10^{-11}	10^{-11}
E_c-E_{trap}(eV)	Acceptor states		
0.2	$8 \cdot 10^{12}$	10^{-18}	10^{-18}
0.4	$7 \cdot 10^{12}$	10^{-13}	10^{-13}
0.6	$6 \cdot 10^{12}$	10^{-11}	10^{-11}

Table 2.1: Values of the interface trap parameters for the acceptor and donor states included in the simulations shown in Fig. 2.6

2.5 INFLUENCE OF STRESS MAGNITUDE AND STRESS TYPE

Results from Sec. 2.3 and 2.4 have shown the relevant role of interface traps and free carriers in the performance of strained silicon devices. However, Pockels effect may still have a contribution in the obtained measurements. To further investigate this possibility, a similar sample was fabricated but this time with an intrinsic stress as large as 2 GPa and being compressive instead of tensile. The fabricated Mach-Zehder interferometers were equal to those of the tensile stress sample but with active lengths of 1 mm, 2 mm and 4 mm and all having the same orientation. The effective index change as a function of the applied voltage is shown in Fig. 2.7 (a) for the fabricated structures. Contrary to the expected results, the compressively strained structures show a similar effective index change, if not weaker, compared to those of the tensile sample even though the stress is around 5 times more intense. This is clearly seen in Fig. 2.7 (b), where the elecro-optic performance of two Mach-Zehnder interferometers with compressive and tensile stress is shown. Moreover, the change in the stress sign (or stress type) seems to not be affecting the electro-optic performance. This would either indicate that Pockels effect does not play a determinant role on the results or, on the other hand, that tensile stress is a much more efficient way to enhance the Pockels effect. Finally, a less intense hysteresis effect is observed in the compressively stressed devices. Such difference could indicate a change in the interface traps due to the different fabrication process followed for each sample.

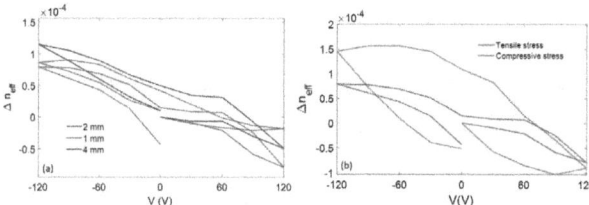

Figure 2.7: Experimental results for the devices under compressive stress and comparison with those subjected to tensile stress. (a) Experimental refractive index change for the fabricated Mach-Zehnder interferometers under 2 GPa of compressive stress and (b) a comparison between the effective index change measured for the 1 mm length devices under compressive and tensile stress.

2.6 EFFECT OF A THERMAL ANNEALING

As a final step in the analysis of the electro-optic response of the strained silicon devices, an annealing process was applied to both fabricated samples. This step made possible the analysis of the same structures but with different stress magnitudes, ruling out the influence of any other source of uncertainty. The annealing process was carried out by heating the samples at 500 ºC during 30 min in atmospheric environment, resulting in a stress variation in both cases. The intrinsic stress before and after annealing was determined via wafer bow measurements, obtaining values after the annealing of -1.25 GPa and 530MPa for the compressive and tensile samples, respectively. That is, the stress in the compressive sample decreased in a 40% while for the tensile sample increased in a 26%. To evaluate the effect of these changes on the strain in the waveguide core, FEM simulations have been carried out. Figure 2.8(a) shows the $\frac{\partial \varepsilon_{xx}}{\partial x}$ strain gradient for the compressive sample before annealing and Fig. 2.8(b) after annealing. Analogously, Fig. 2.8(c) and Fig .2.8(d) show the results for the tensile sample before and after annealing respectively. In addition, as a way of evaluating the impact of the stress variation, the overlap between the strain gradient and the TE fundamental mode has been calculated using the following figure of merit[5]:

$$FOM = \frac{\int_{A_0} e(r_\perp, \omega) \cdot \sum_{i,j} |\frac{\partial \varepsilon_{ii}}{\partial x_j}| \cdot e^*(r_\perp, \omega) dA}{\int n^2(r_\perp, \omega) |e^*(r_\perp, \omega)| dA} \quad (2.2)$$

where $e(r_\perp, \omega)$ refers to the electric field distribution of the optical mode in the silicon waveguide, ε_{ii} are the main strain components with i,j=1,2 or 3 and $n(r_\perp, \omega)$ is the refractive index of silicon in the waveguide cross section. The annealing process has opposite effects for the tensile and compressive cases. While in the first one the stress is clearly increased and the FOM is improved ($\frac{FOM_{after}}{FOM_{before}} \approx 1.24$), the overlap integral is decreased in the second case ($\frac{FOM_{after}}{FOM_{before}} \approx 0.62$). Therefore, if the Pockels effect would play a measurable role, these changes should be reflected in the electro-optic performance, which is shown in Fig. 2.9 (a) for the compressive sample and in Fig. 2.9 (b) for the tensile case.

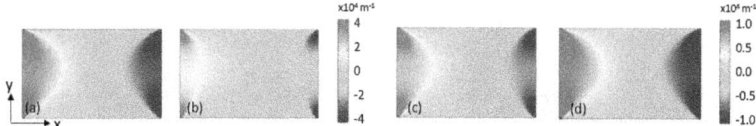

Figure 2.8: Effect of the annealing on the strain inside the structures. Simulated strain gradient $\frac{\partial \varepsilon_{xx}}{\partial x}$ for: the compressive stress sample (a) before and (b) after the annealing process, tensile stress sample (c) before and (d) after the annealing process. The annealing was performed at 500°C during 30 minutes in atmospheric environment.

By contrary, the electro-optic results show either almost no difference, in the tensile case, or even the opposite effect to that expected for Pockels effect in the compressive case. While the stress has significantly decreased in the compressive structures after annealing, the maximum Δn_{eff} has even slightly increase. The explanation to the observed results must have, therefore, another origin. Indeed, the effective index change for the sample with compressive stress (Fig. 2.9(a)) shows the characteristic peak and a completely analogous curve to that obtained in the simulations but for lower concentrations of positive fixed charge.

In fact, the positive fixed charge near in the silicon nitride layer arises primarily from nitride and silicon dangling bonds (the so called N and K centers). The amount of this fixed charge and also the amount of interface traps can be strongly affected during annealing processes. Different studies have reported the passivation/depassivation of bulk defects due to hydrogen diffusion into the silicon nitride films after a heating process[78,79]. Dangling bonds can be neutralized either by healing Si-N bonds or by an hydrogen atom, which creates new

N-H and Si-H bonds and causes the decrease of the fixed charge in the film. The opposite, meaning a dehydrogenation of the silicon nitride layer, would lead to an increase of dangling bonds and fixed charge if no more Si-N bonds are created instead.

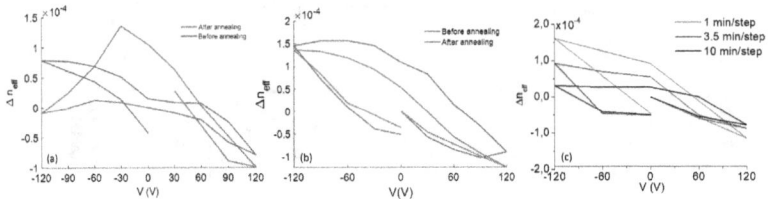

Figure 2.9: Experimental results for the compressive and tensile stress samples under different annealing and time measurement conditions. Comparison of results before and after the annealing for (a) the compressive and (b) tensile samples. (c) Results for the sample with tensile stress after annealing as a function of different times steps per each voltage measurement. The annealing process was performed at 500°C during 30 minutes in atmospheric environment.

Therefore, a significant passivation of dangling bonds could have occurr in the compressive sample due to the annealing process, leading to a decrease in the total amount of fixed charge. On the other hand, a linear behaviour is still found for the tensile stressed devices, which could mean a lack of defect healing during the annealing in this case. In order to confirm the relationship between the reduction of fixed charge and defect passivation, Raman measurements have been carried out for both samples before and after the annealing. These results are more exhaustively detailed in the following section.

2.7 Raman measurements

The spectral positions of the Raman peaks correspond to the vibrational frequencies of the molecules in the film. Position, area and width give information about atomic composition and bond arrangements.

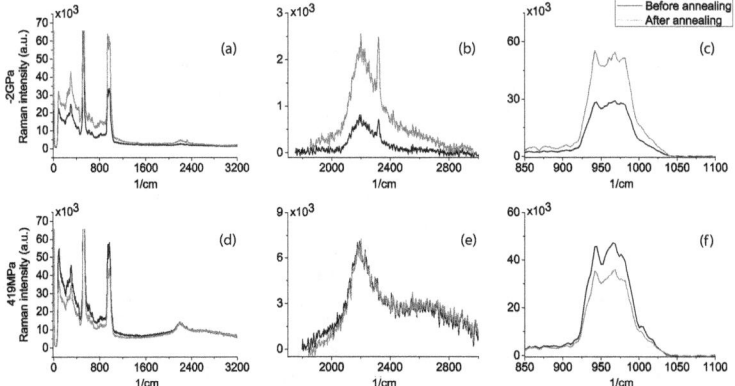

Figure 2.10: Raman spectra. Top Figures show Raman spectra obtained for the compressive stress sample, where (a) shows the complete Raman spectra and Figures (b) and (c) show a zoom on the range where peaks related to Si-H and Si-N bonds are located respectively. Analogously, (d) shows the complete Raman spectra for the 420 MPa sample and Figures (e) and (f) show a zoom on Si-H, Si-N related peaks.

Raman results are depicted in Fig. 2.10 where the peaks related to the Si-H and Si-N bonds have been zoomed for clarity. Peaks have been identified by means of a Lorentzian fitting. Area and peak position are shown in Tables 2.2 and 2.3. Results show a great increase in the area of the Si-H and Si-N peaks for the compressive sample, especially the area of the Si-H(N_3) bond has increased ∼24 times, which indicates a film hydrogenation and experimentally confirms the initial hypothesis of a positive fixed charge decrease due to the heating process.

	Vibration type	Before annealing	
		Centre (cm^{-1})	Area (10^5 cm^{-2})
Compressive	Si-H(N_2Si)	2205.1	1.61
	Si-H(N_3)	2321.1	0.157
	Si-N bending	972.1	18.6
	Si-N stretching 1	942.3	6.59
	Si-N streshing 2	822.9	4.59
Tensile	Si-H(N_2Si)	2198.9	26.7
	Si-H(N_x)	2625.2	16.5
	Si-N bending	970.4	30.1
	Si-N stretching 1	941.3	9.80
	Si-N streching 2	822.7	7.64
		After annealing	
Compressive	Si-H(N_2Si)	2188.6	2.81
	Si-H(N_3)	2301.1	3.75
	Si-N bending	972.4	34.2
	Si-N stretching	942.5	12.2
	Si-N streshing 2	822.5	10.1
Tensile	Si-H(N_2Si)	2198.8	25.8
	Si-H(N_x)	2620.5	25.1
	Si-N bending	971.2	22.1
	Si-N stretching 1	941.9	7.89
	Si-N streching 2	823.0	6.39

Table 2.2: Lorentzian fitting results for the compressive and tensile stress samples before and after the annealing process.

	Si-H(N_2Si)	Si-H(N_3)	Si-N bend	Si-N stretch. 1	Si-N strech. 2
Compressive	1.74	23.9	1.84	1.85	2.20
Tensile	0.97	1.52	0.74	0.80	0.84

Table 2.3: Peak area ratio before and after annealing.

On the other hand, the reason why it was not possible to observe the peak in the tensile sample (Fig. 2.9(b)) is also confirmed by a general slight decrease in the hydrogen content of the film. It is possible to see in Table 2.2 that the area of the Si-N and Si-H bonds has remained almost constant or even decrease (with the exception of a small increase in Si-H(N_x) bonds), which again supports the initial hypothesis.

In addition, a change in the hysteresis effect is found for both samples before and after the annealing (Fig. 2.9(a,b)), which could also be related to the dynamics at the interface. In our results, it seems to be a correlation between higher hydrogenation and a stronger hysteresis[78]. In fact, an increase in the hydrogen bonds at this interface would slow the process of interface trap creation compared to a scenario where most of the dangling bonds are already created, giving rise to an increased hysteresis effect. This is what we observe for the compressive sample after the annealing while the opposite is obtained for the tensile sample, in agreement with the reduction of H revealed by Raman results. The influence of interface trap dynamics was also analyzed by measuring the electro-optical response for different time steps. Figure 2.9(c) shows the effective index change for the tensile sample after anneling taking into account a time step of 1, 3.5 and 10 minutes between each voltage measurement. It can also be seen that longer time steps give rise to smaller effective index changes due to the higher amount of interface traps created.

In , the obtained results confirm that carrier effects can play a prominent role in the performance of strained silicon devices. The trapping properties at the interface between the silicon and silicon nitride have a strong influence on the electro-optic static response. The experimental results supported by simulations indicate that the silicon nitride charge is affected by the trapping of carriers at the interface resulting in a hysteretic response and the possibility of having saturation effects. In all cases, we did not see any correlation between the electro-optic response and the magnitude of the applied stress which precludes a significant contribution of the Pockels effect. By contrary, the measured electro-optic response was consistent with variations of the silicon nitride fixed charge and the interface trapping properties, which was also confirmed by Raman measurements.

2.8 SECOND HARMONIC GENERATION EXPERIMENTS

In Secs. 2.3-2.7 the influence of free carriers and interface traps in the electro-optic behavior of strained silicon Mach-Zehnder interferometers has been analysed, demonstrating a major contribution of these effects in their performance. Those results, therefore, are inconclusive about the existence of Pockels effect in the fabricated structures, pointing to a very weak second-order nonlinear effect, if present. In this context, second harmonic generation emerges as an accurate tool to detect and discriminate the origin of the non-linear processes taking place because the influence of free carriers can be ruled out. In fact, several works have been published measuring second harmonic generation (SHG) in strained silicon waveguides and have estimated values for the $\chi^{(2)}$ coefficient in the order of a few pm/V. More recently, the contribution of electric-field induced second harmonic generation (EFISH) in those results has been pointed out[19]. The role of crystallographic orientation, however, was not explored in these measurements, which could be used as a distinctive feature to distinguish any contribution of the strained induced $\chi^{(2)}$ in the output signal. With this aim, second harmonic generation experiments were designed and performed in the context of an internship at the Nanoscience Laboratory of the University of Trento. The experimental setup is first detailed out in Sec. 2.8.1 together with a theoretical description of the phenomena in Sec.

2.8.2. The design of the fabricated structures is then presented in 2.8.3 and the experimental results in 2.8.4.

2.8.1 EXPERIMENTAL SETUP

The experimental setup used to perform the second-harmonic measurements is shown in Fig. 2.11. The source is an continuous wavelength laser (IPG Photonics CLPF ®) with an average maximum output power of 4 W. It works in the spectral range from 2200 nm to 2600 nm with a pulse duration of 30 fs. The pump signal is then passed through a polarizer step constituted by a half waveplate followed by a quarter waveplate and finally sent to a colimator to couple it to a lensed fiber.

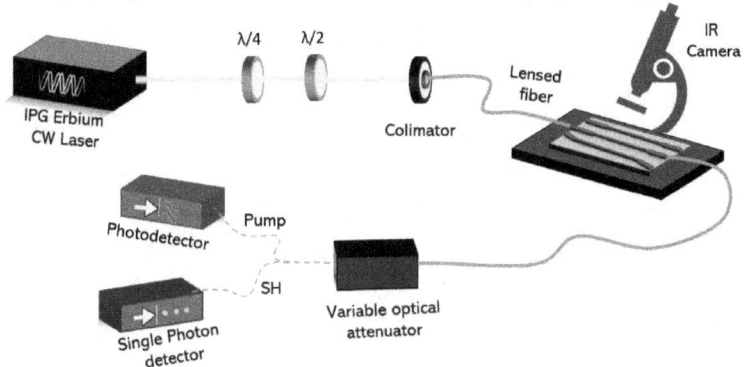

Figure 2.11: Second-harmoic generation setup. Sketch of the setup used to perform the second-harmonic generation measurements.

After passing through the test structure the light is coupled again to a lensed fiber. A NIR-VIS camera (FIND-R-SCOPE-85700 ®) is used for the alignment step with the aid of an auxiliar beam at telecom wavelegths, which is visible with the camera and is good for a rough alignment. The beam at telecom wavelength is then substituted by the pump beam at 2.3 μm finishing the alignment by maximizing the output power. The output signal is carried to a variable optical attenuator (VOA) which can be used in case the output power excceeds the limit of the photodetector. In the detection step, either the pump or the SH signal can be measured. In case the pump signal wants to be measured, the output fiber at the VOA is connected to an extended InGaAs photodiode which has a responsivity in the range from 900 nm to 2600 nm. On the other hand, if the SH pulse wants to be measured, a single photon detector is used, an InGaAs single photon avalanche photodiode (ID-Quantique-ID201 ®) with a detection efficiency from 10% to 25% in the wavelength working range of the second-harmonic signal (from 1100 nm to 1200 nm). The average power detected by the single photon detector can be calculated from the relation

$$< P_{sh} > = \frac{hc}{\lambda_{sh}} \frac{C - C_{DC}}{\eta} \qquad (2.3)$$

where C is the counts given by the photodetector, η its detection efficiency, C_{DC} the dark counting rate, h the plank constant and c the velocity of light.

2.8.2 THEORETICAL DESCRIPTION

To model the second harmonic generation in our silicon waveguides, we will consider negligible the effect of third-order nonlinearities such as self-phase modulation (SPM) and cross-phase modulation (XPM). We will take as well the continuous-wave approximation which allows us to neglect the temporal derivatives [17,19]. Finally, because of the weakness of the effects we are considering, we will have a small generation efficiency and the pump pulse will not be affected by the generated second harmonic (SH) pulses. All these approximations make possible to write the total SH power generated in the silicon structures in a simple manner:

$$P_{sh} = P_p^2 |\gamma_{sh}^{(2)}|^2 L^2 sinc^2\left(\frac{\Delta\beta L}{2}\right) \quad (2.4)$$

which depends quadratically on the pump power and the length of the structure and through the *sinc* function with the phase mismatch $\Delta\beta = (2\beta_p - \beta_{sh})$. The coefficient $\gamma_{sh}^{(2)}$ is related to the group index of the pump and SH modes and the interaction of them with the non-linear material:

$$\gamma_{sh}^{(2)} = \omega_{sh} \frac{n_{G,p}\sqrt{n_{G,sh}}}{\sqrt{8 A_0 \varepsilon_0 c^3}} \Gamma^{(2)} \quad (2.5)$$

where A_0 is the area of the waveguide cross section and $\Gamma^{(2)}$ is defined by

$$\Gamma^{(2)} = \frac{\sqrt{A_0} \int e(r_\perp,\omega_p) \chi^{(2)} : e^*(r_\perp,\omega_{sh}) e(r_\perp,\omega_p) dA}{\left(\int n^2(r_\perp,\omega_p)|e(r_\perp,\omega_p)|^2 dA\right)\sqrt{\int n^2(r_\perp,\omega_{sh})|e(r_\perp,\omega_{sh})|^2 dA}} \quad (2.6)$$

being $n(r_\perp,\omega_i)$ the refractive index distribution in the plane A_∞ perpendicular to the propagation direction at frequency ω_i.

Thus, based on Eq. 2.4 the power at the second harmonic is maximized when $\Delta\beta = 0$, i.e. when the phase of the pump and second-harmonic signal are matched. Considering that $\beta_i = \frac{2\pi n_{eff,i}}{\lambda}$ and that $\lambda_p = 2\lambda_{sh}$, we get that the phase-matching condition is achieved when

$$n_{eff,sh} = n_{eff,p} \quad (2.7)$$

That is, when the pump and SH modes have the same effective index when propagating through the structure, which can be achieved through intermodal phase-matching.

2.8.3   Design of the strained silicon waveguides

The design of the structures have to be done obeying certain restrictions coming from the characteristics of silicon, the available wafers and the silicon nitride fabrication process. In fact, the intrinsic stress of the silicon nitride layer increases with larger thickness, thus, a 700 nm thick layer was deposited through a PECVD process to reach a large compressive stress of 2 GPa. Higher intrinsic stresses led to cracking of the wafer and were not possible to achieve in practice. A SOI wafer with a 3 μm thick BOX and a (100) silicon layer of 250 nm was used to fabricate the structures. A sketch of the waveguides cross-section is shown in Fig. 2.12 (a). Different orientations, ranging from 0º to 45º were used to detect the presence of any rotational dependency. A wider waveguide of 4 μm is used at the beggining and the end of the structure and is then tapered to a narrower part of length L and width w, which can be rotated an angle ϕ with respect to the [100] axis of silicon. A sketch of the design is depicted in 2.12 (b). This is done due to two main reasons. First, a wider width eases the coupling of light from and to the fiber. Secondly, the wider the waveguide, the less strain is induced in its core. In this manner, the "active" part of the structure, i.e. the part that shows nonlinearities, is only the narrower that is going to be designed in the following and, in addition, this length L is maintained constant regardless of its rotation angle ϕ. The inset in 2.12 (b) shows the horizontal strain component ε_{xx} inside the narrow (top) and the wider input/output waveguides (bottom).

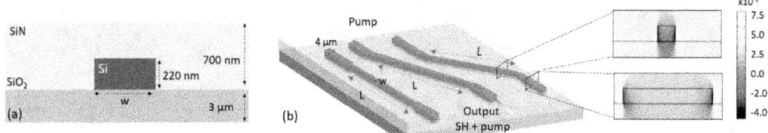

Figure 2.12: Design of the strained silicon waveguides. (a) Sketch of the waveguide cross-section showing the structure dimensions and the design parameters, (b) Sketch of the fabricated structures. The insets show the ε_{xx} inside the narrow (top) and wider input/output waveguides (bottom).

The pump signal was chosen to be operated at a wavelength around 2.3 μm so that two photon absorption (TPA) is negligible and the pump power can be increased without increasing losses. In addition, it is convenient that the second-harmonic signal is generated in the transparent spectral silicon region, i.e. with pump wavelengths above 2.2 μm.

The length of the active part of the waveguide was designed to achieve a compromise between optical losses, which increase with decreasing widths, induced strain in the waveguide core, which also increases with decreasing widths, and to maximize the coefficient $\Gamma^{(2)}$. Therefore, waveguide widths below 700 nm were not considered to avoid excessive optical losses. As shown in Fig. 2.13, there are different modes at the second-harmonic wavelength that fulfill the phase-matching condition above this value, such as TE_4, TM_3 or TE_5. The magnetic mode was chosen due to two reasons. Firstly, the associated waveguide width is the lowest of the three options, which maximizes the strain and, hence, it should theoretically maximize strain induced $\chi^{(2)}$. In addition, if we assume a constant value for the strain induced $\chi^{(2)}$ as also done in [17], we can take out this value from the integral in $\Gamma^{(2)}$, leaving:

$$F.O.M. = \frac{\sqrt{A_0} \int e(r_\perp, \omega_p) e^*(r_\perp, \omega_{sh}) e(r_\perp, \omega_p) dA}{\left(\int n^2(r_\perp, \omega_p) |e(r_\perp, \omega_p)|^2 dA\right) \sqrt{\int n^2(r_\perp, \omega_{sh}) |e(r_\perp, \omega_{sh})|^2 dA}} \quad (2.8)$$

which is basically a figure of merit measuring the overlap between the pump and SH mode, similar to that of Eq. 2.2. Moreover, as it is known that $\chi^{(2)}$ should be dependent on the strain gradients, an analogous figure of merit to that of Eq. 2.2 can be calculated for the overlap between pump and SH modes and strain:

$$F.O.M.(\varepsilon) = \frac{\sqrt{A_0} \int e(r_\perp, \omega_p) \cdot \sum_{i,j} \left|\frac{\partial \varepsilon_{ii}}{\partial x_j}\right| \cdot e^*(r_\perp, \omega_{sh}) e(r_\perp, \omega_p) dA}{\left(\int n^2(r_\perp, \omega_p) |e(r_\perp, \omega_p)|^2 dA\right) \sqrt{\int n^2(r_\perp, \omega_{sh}) |e(r_\perp, \omega_{sh})|^2 dA}} \quad (2.9)$$

where i,j = 1,2 and 3.

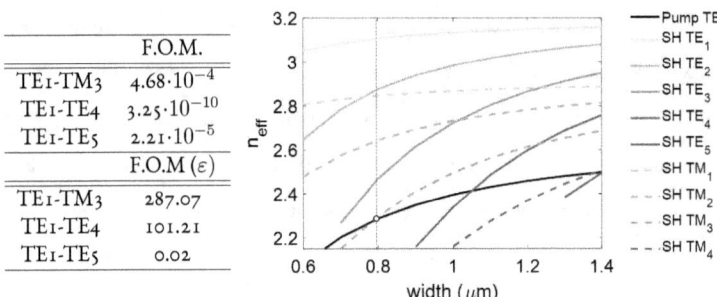

	F.O.M.
TE1-TM3	$4.68 \cdot 10^{-4}$
TE1-TE4	$3.25 \cdot 10^{-10}$
TE1-TE5	$2.21 \cdot 10^{-5}$
	F.O.M (ε)
TE1-TM3	287.07
TE1-TE4	101.21
TE1-TE5	0.02

Figure 2.13: Phase-matching as a function of waveguide width. Effective refractive index as a function of the waveguide width for the pump TE mode at 2.3 μm and the second-harmonic TE and TM modes at 1.15 μm

The value of both figure of merits has been calculated for the three different modal combinations, as shown in the aggregated table to Fig. 2.13, demonstrating that the highest overlap in both cases is achieved for the TM$_3$ combination. Finally, TM modes for the pump signal are not shown in Fig. 2.13 because they are not supported for the considered widths. Figure 2.14 (a) shows a more detailed view of the phase matching condition for the TE$_1$-TM$_3$ combination, revealing that the exact phase-matching wavelength is located at 2.3215 μm and an effective index of 2.221. The normalized second harmonic efficiency that should be observed in the experimental measurements is also shown in Fig. 2.14 (b).

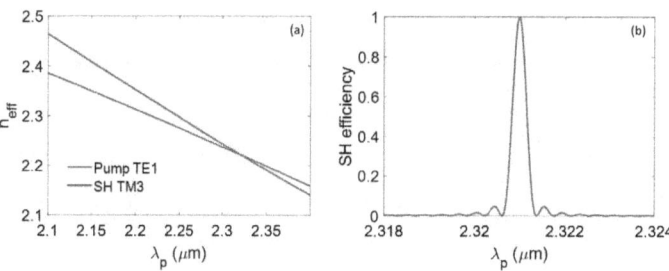

Figure 2.14: Predicted second-harmonic generation. (a) Phase-matching condition for the TE1-TM3 intermodal combination and (b) normalized second-harmonic response.

From Eq. 2.4 the generated signal depends quadratically on the waveguide length, the pump power and the second-order susceptibility. We could, therefore, estimate an effective $\chi^{(2)}$ analysing the generated SH power in the fabricated structures. Figure 2.15 (a) shows the generated SH power as a function of the waveguide length for the designed structures and considering a pump average power of 5 mW and a second-order susceptiblity of 1 pm/V. On Fig. 2.15 (b), on the other hand, the SH signal is shown for three different lengths (1 mm, 2 mm and 3 mm) as a function of the pump average power.

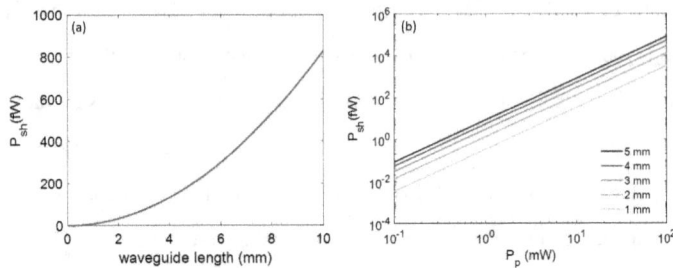

Figure 2.15: SHG as a function of length and pump power. Second-harmonic power as a function of (a) waveguide length with an average pump power of 5mW and (b) average pump power for different lengths.

Based on Figs. 2.15 (a) and (b) and considering that the length of the fabricated waveguides is of 3 mm, we should expect values for the collected SH power on the order of several fW for pump powers in the order of mW, whenever an effective second order susceptibility of about 1 pm/V is present. Figure 2.16 shows the dependency of the SH power with this parameter. In fact, effective $\chi^{(2)}$ values below 0.1 pm/V would produce SH powers below the fW range, which is the detection limit of the setup.

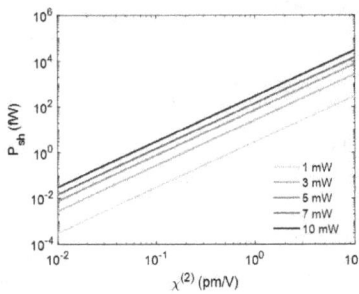

Figure 2.16: SHG as a function of the effective second order susceptibility for different input pump powers.

In addition, it is important for the considered experiment to take into account the rotational dependency of the strain and, therefore, of the photoelastic effect, to rule out any possible influence if any change with ϕ is experimentally observed. Figure 2.17 (a) shows the change in the phase-matching condition for the TE1-TM3 modes as a function of ϕ, demonstrating an almost negligible shift of several nm. On the other hand, if a change in SH efficiency is experimentally observed, some of it could be attributed due to a different overlap of the strain with the optical modes due to photoelastic effect. As shown in Fig. 2.17 (b), this influence can also be discarded as the induced changes are in all cases below 1%.

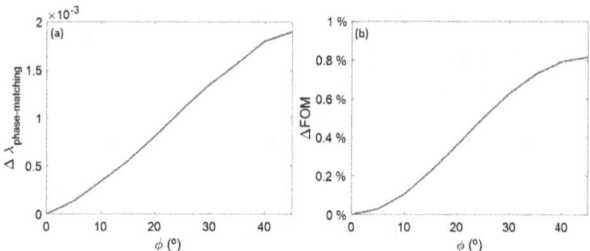

Figure 2.17: Influence of photoelastic effect. Change in the (a) phase matching condition and (b) figure of merit due to photoelastic effect. Values have been calculated with respect to the value at 0°.

2.8.4　Experimental results

Figure 2.18 shows the experimentally measured pump power as a function of the input wavelength for the waveguides with an active length of 3 mm. In addition, the exact value at the phase-matching wavelength is given in the aggregated Table. The variation in the measured pump power for the differently oriented waveguides is attributed to a difference in the coupling losses.

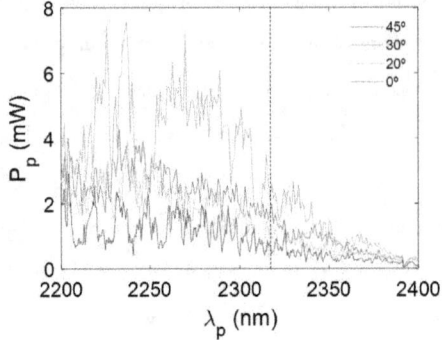

Figure 2.18: Measured pump power for the fabricated structures. Measured pump power as a function of wavelength for the waveguides oriented at 0°, 20°,30° and 45°. The aggregated Table shows the power at the phase matching wavelength, also marked with a dashed line in the Figure.

Therefore, the expected SH power has been calculated for each structure considering the pump power extracted from Fig. 2.18, obtaining values in the fW range if considering an effective $\chi^{(2)}$ of 1 pm/V. The exact values are shown in Table 2.4.

ϕ	$P_{sh}^{expected}$
0º	1.11 fW
20º	1.64 fW
30º	15.94 fW
45º	4.67 fW

Table 2.4: Expected second-harmonic power for the fabricated structures. The values have been calculated considering a $\chi^{(2)}$ of 1 pm/V and the pump power extracted from Fig. 2.18 at the phase matching wavelength.

On the contrary, the spectral response measured for the SH signal shows no evidence of second harmonic generation for any crystallographic orientation, as reflected in Fig. 2.18.

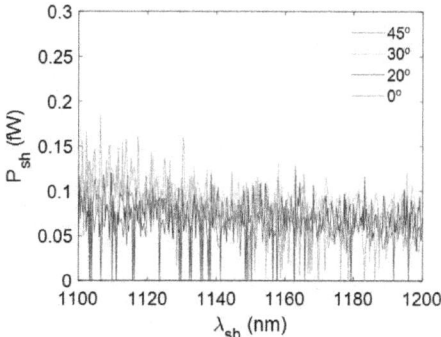

Figure 2.19: Measured second-harmonic power. Experimental second-harmonic power measured for the waveguides oriented at 0°, 20°,30° and 45°.

The above results set an upper limit for the effective second-order susceptibility of ∼0.1 pm/V, taking 0.15 fW as the detection limit. Furthermore, optical losses of about 10 dB/cm were measured for the pump signal. If we consider approximately the same values for the second-harmonic one, the upper limit for the effective strain induced $\chi^{(2)}$ slightly increases to ∼0.3 pm/V. However, it is important to highlight that a low effective second-order susceptibility does not necessarily mean the absence of strain induced $\chi^{(2)}$. In fact, as shown in Fig. 2.20, the distribution of the strain gradient inside the silicon waveguide is completely anti-symmetric, thus, areas with opposite signs could be counteracting each other, resulting in a low or even null value for $\chi^{(2)}$.

Such point will be addressed in Chapter 4, where a p-i-n junction and a Si-SiGe structure are explored to avoid those unwanted effects.

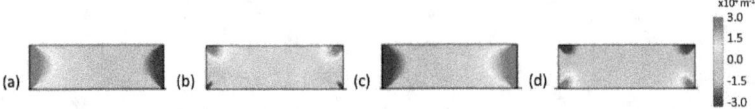

Figure 2.20: Strain gradients. (a) $\frac{\partial \varepsilon_{xx}}{\partial x}$ (b) $\frac{\partial \varepsilon_{xx}}{\partial y}$, (c) $\frac{\partial \varepsilon_{yy}}{\partial x}$ and (d) $\frac{\partial \varepsilon_{yy}}{\partial y}$ strain components inside the 800 nm silicon waveguide.

3

Exploitation of the observed features: an electro-optic memory

ALTHOUGH THE NON-VOLATILE MEMORY is a crucial functionality for a wide range of applications in photonic integrated circuits, it still poses a challenge in silicon photonic technology. Related to this issue, we have been dealing with the trapping properties of silicon nitride in Chapter 2. Such properties were considered a disadvantage in that case, however, if correctly managed, they can be exploited to implement a non-volatile device, similarly to how it is done in the microelectronic industry with the SONOS (silicon-oxide-nitride-oxide-silicon) memory cell. In this Chapter, therefore, a similar approach to that of microelectronic memories is taken, although the silicon nitride has been replaced by a hafnium oxide layer. The device is proposed for enabling a programmable erasable photonic memory fully compatible with the silicon platform.

This chapter is divided in two main sections. First, an overview of the state-of-the-art of non-volatile memory effect in silicon is provided. After that, an approach for enabling a fast electro-optic memory working in the microsecond range is discussed. In the following section the design of the charge trapping structure is detailed and, finally, the non-volatile phase shifter is integrated into a ring resonator.

3.1 Non-volatile memory effect in silicon.

Silicon technology has gradually emerged as the platform of choice when it comes to developing photonic integrated circuits (PICs) due to its potential integration with electronic circuits in the same chip and the possibility of reusing the mature and cost-effective manufacturing infrastructure of the microelectronic industry. In addition, silicon has excellent properties for the development of photonic devices such as high thermal conductivity, high optical damage threshold and the presence of third-order non-linearities [55]. Furthermore, the large index contrast between silicon and silica makes the SOI technology a great candidate for developing compact devices. The presence of Raman and Kerr effects joined to the high optical density coming from the large index contrast has made possible optical amplification [25,60,71], lasing [71,99,100], and wavelength conversion [36,69,131], in the silicon platform. However, the non-volatile electro-optical memory, which is a crucial functionality demanded by a wide range of applications such as efficient data storage, is still a challenge in this platform. Several solutions have been proposed to overcome this issue, some of those relying on the integration of new materials [89,97,101,126], however, they come with the drawback of not using the standard fabrication process flow of the CMOS industry. On the other hand, a solution for a programmable erasable memory that exploits plasma dispersion effect has been proposed based on a floating gate scheme [111,112]. Despite the good outcomes of the device, it has some limitations coming from the chosen technology and the complexity of the structure. In fact, the scaling of the tunneling layer is a key issue in floating gate memories: as a consequence of the conductive nature of the polysilicon floating gate, complete memory discharge is caused whenever there is a fabrication defect in the thin tunnel oxide [96,118]. This issue has been overcome in the microelectronic industry by replacing the floating gate by a charge trapping dielectric such as silicon nitride [96,118]. In photonics, two works have been reported to date following this approach [8,40], however, the voltages needed for discharging the device exceed 100 V. In fact, the most recent one [40] is oriented to ring-resonator trimming instead of memory applications due to the need of UV (ultraviolet) light in order to charge the device. A of the state-of-the-art of non-volatile silicon memory devices following a similar approach to that taken in this work is provided in Table 3.1.

Technology	V_{write}	V_{erase}	t_{write}	t_{erase}	Ref.
SONOS	10 V	100 V	1 s	2 s	8
SONOS	120 V	N/A	$\sim$ ms	N/A	40
Floating gate	20 V	6 V	600 ms	225 ms	111,112

Table 3.1: State-of-the-art in silicon non-volatile photonic memory devices

3.2 A non-volatile photonic memory based on a SAHAS configuration

Conventional SONOS memories are essentially a MOS (metal-oxide-silicon) transistor where the metal has been replaced by a highly doped ($\sim 10^{20} cm^{-3}$) polysilicon gate and the gate oxide by a ONO (oxide-nitride-oxide) dielectric stack, as shown in Fig. 3.1(a). The dielectric placed in the middle of the stack, usually silicon nitride, is used to capture the carriers injected from the silicon channel. When trying to reuse this concept for a photonic memory, the ONO stack is placed over the silicon waveguide. Once the silicon nitride is charged by applying a positive voltage to the gate, carriers will accumulate in the waveguide border to screen the stored charge and will change the effective index of the guided photonic mode due to the plasma dispersion effect in silicon. A sketch of the concept is depicted in Fig. 3.1 (b). However, this configuration comes with several limitations arising, among other factors, from the low overlap between the guided photonic mode and the accumulated charges, which limits the effective index change achieved for a given carrier accumulation. To overcome these restrictions, the configuration shown in Fig. 3.1(c) named as SAHAS (silicon-aluminum-Hafnium-aluminum-silicon) is proposed. In this structure, the relatively low doped polysilicon gate acts as part of the guiding structure, placing the core of the optical mode right on top of the charge accumulation. In addition, this configuration allows for a direct voltage application because the gate is placed next to the thin ONO stack and reduces the voltage needed for the erasing process.

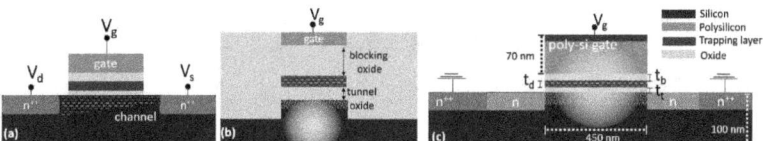

Figure 3.1: Sketch of (a) a conventional SONOS memory, (b) SONOS photonic structure used in [8,40] and (c) proposed structure. Sketches are shown not to scale.

3.2.1 DESIGN OF THE CHARGE TRAPPING STRUCTURE

The dimensions of the proposed SAHAS waveguide structure (Fig. 3.1(c)) have been designed to optimize the TE polarized optical mode overlap with the carrier accumulation layer. Consequently, gate and slab thicknesses of 70 nm and 100 nm, respectively, have been selected together with a polysilicon width of 450 nm. Moreover, Al_2O_3 has been chosen as the tunnel and blocking oxides due to its higher dielectric constant ($\epsilon_r \sim 9$ [98]) compared to silica and HfO_2 as the charge storage layer due to its high trap density ranging between $10^{20} cm^{-3}$ and $10^{21} cm^{-3}$ [128]. Both materials ensure CMOS compatibility. Drain and source have been heavily doped (n^{++}-type $10^{20} cm^{-3}$) to avoid the creation of a Schottky contact and placed 300 nm away from the poly-silicon waveguide to minimize optical losses. A more lightly doped area (n-type $5 \cdot 10^{18} cm^{-3}$) is extended right next to the polysilicon, as shown in Fig. 3.1(c). Analogously, the gate has also a highly doped thickness of 20 nm on the top ($10^{19} cm^{-3}$). Soref equations have been used to obtain the index (Δn) and absorption ($\Delta \alpha$) changes due to the plasma dispersion effect in silicon and polysilicon at λ=1.55 μm [70]:

$$\Delta n = -8.88 \cdot 10^{-22} \Delta N - 8.5 \cdot 10^{-18} \Delta P^{0.8} \quad (3.1)$$

$$\Delta \alpha = 8.5 \cdot 10^{-18} \Delta N - 6.0 \cdot 10^{-18} \Delta P \quad (3.2)$$

where ΔN and ΔP are, respectively, the electron and hole concentrations. In addition, optical losses of 20 dB/cm have been considered for the polysilicon material[3].

SILVACO[6] has been also used to analyze and design the electrical and optical performance of the structure. This software calculates the tunneling currents through the dielectric stack self consistently and obtains the structure behavior by solving Poisson's and charge continuity equations numerically. The dielectric stack has been modeled as a wide band gap semiconductor and direct and Fowler-Nordheim tunneling currents have been considered to compute the solution. The Poole-Frenkel effect as well as trap-assisted tunneling are known to control the retention behavior of this kind of structures[64,83,84,88,117] and have also been included to simulate this process. Nevertheless, it is important to highlight that the retention characteristics are also influenced by the creation of extrinsic defects in the tunnel oxide, which cannot be considered through simulation models and makes specially important to control the oxide quality during the fabrication process. In addition, the MOS parameter, which enables Shockley-Read-Hall (SRH), Fermi Statistics (FERMI), and the Lombardi Mobility model (CVT) for transverse field and concentration mobility dependence has been used. All these mechanisms and models are included in the ATLAS package from SILVACO[6]. The values for the parameters involved in the simulations are specified in Table 3.2.

The main variables that will influence the tunneling currents, i.e. electric fields E_1 and

	Symbol	Quantity	Value
HfO$_2$	N_T (cm^{-3})	trap density	$5 \cdot 10^{20}$
	ϕ_d (eV)	trap depth	1.5
	ε_r	dielectric constant	22
	χ (eV)	electron affinity	2.0
Al$_2$O$_3$	Refractive index		5.8
	m*	electron effective mass	0.4
	ε_r		4
	χ (eV)	electron affinity	14.4
	E_{gap} (eV)	gap energy	8.8

Table 3.2: Main parameters used for the electrical simulations

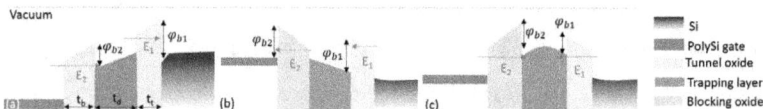

Figure 3.2: Band diagram of the (a) writing, (b) erasing and (c) retention processes.

E_2, blocking (t_b) and tunneling (t_t) oxide thicknesses and tunneling barriers φ_{b1} and φ_{b2} seen by the electrons, are depicted in the band diagrams of Fig. 3.2 for the (a) writing, (b) erasing and (c) retention processes. When a voltage is applied to the gate, an electric field will be created along the dielectric stack. Consequently, there will be two tunneling currents: the desired one through the tunneling oxide to charge and discharge the HfO$_2$ layer and an unwanted current through the blocking oxide that will inject carriers from and to the gate. Another current, governed by the Poole-Frenkel effect and trap assisted tunneling, will be in charge of moving the electrons across the HfO$_2$ layer hopping from trap to trap[117]. The design parameters are detailed in Table 3.3. A thickness of 6 nm has been designed for the tunneling oxide, which enables the writing process but, at the same time, avoids excessive charge loss during the retention period. Regarding the charge trapping layer, a HfO$_2$ thickness of 4 nm has been selected together with a blocking oxide of 6 nm, which prevents the back tunneling of the trapped carriers.

Table 3.3: Main parameters used for the electrical simulations

Symbol	Quantity	Value
t_b (nm)	blocking oxide thickness	6
t_t (nm)	tunneling oxide thickness	6
t_d (nm)	trapping layer thickness	4

On the other hand, the writing/erasing speed and stored charge will also heavily depend on the doping levels of the silicon slab and polysilicon gate. To better illustrate the situation, Figs. 3.3(a) and (c) show, respectively, the potential across the structure for the writing (V_g = 21.5 V) and erasing (V_g = -30 V) processes for a p-type slab and gate with doping concentrations of $10^{16} cm^{-3}$. Figure 3.3(b) and (d) show the voltage across a vertical line at the center of the structure during the writing and erasing steps, respectively, for doping levels of $10^{16} cm^{-3}$ and $5 \cdot 10^{18} cm^{-3}$. For the writing state, majority carriers easily accumulate on both sides of the dielectric stack and all the applied voltage drops along the dielectrics. However, at the erasing process, minority carriers are not enough to screen the required voltage and a resistive path appears between gate and source/drain. As a consequence, the voltage falls in the semiconductor materials instead of falling in the tunnel oxide and strongly hinders the discharge process, especially for the low doped structure. By using a higher doping concentration for gate and slab ($5 \cdot 10^{18} cm^{-3}$), we can improve the performance and a drop of 4 V is achieved inside the tunnel oxide.

Once the carrier and voltage distribution are known, the writing and erasing processes of the HfO_2 layer can be calculated and, by using Soref's equations 3.1 and 3.2, we can translate the stored charge to an effective index change of the optical mode. In fact, a key feature is the amount of stored charge needed to achieve a given effective index change. This result is shown in Fig. 3.4 for different gate and slab doping concentrations, demonstrating

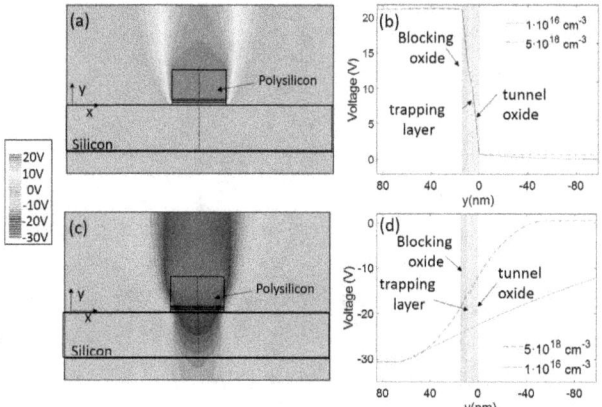

Figure 3.3: Contour plot of the potential across the device for (a) the writing state at V_g = 21.5 V and (c) the erasing state at V_g = -30 V considering a low doped structure ($10^{16} cm^{-3}$). Voltage drop along the vertical line depicted in the contour plots for (b) the writing state at V_g =21.5 V and (d) the erasing state at V_g = -30 V for a low ($1 \cdot 10^{16} cm^{-3}$) and highly ($5 10^{18} cm^{-3}$) doped structure.

an approximately linear relationship between both parameters. Moreover, the lower are the doping concentrations of the structure, less charge is needed to achieve the same effective index change and optical losses will also decrease. Thereby, a trade-off must be achieved between the low doping approach and a faster programming/erase processes of a highly doped structure.

Using a doping concentration of $5 \cdot 10^{18} cm^{-3}$ for the gate and slightly adjusting it to $3 \cdot 10^{18} cm^{-3}$ at the slab, the writing process can be completed by applying a voltage of 21.5 V to the gate. A maximum stored charge of $7 \cdot 10^{-15}$ C/μm is achieved, as shown in Fig. 3.5(a), which is equivalent to an effective index change of $1.5 \cdot 10^{-3}$. The erasing state is accomplished by applying -30 V. Both, writing and erasing processes, are achieved within a 100 μs time range, however, a small residual charge of around $0.6 \cdot 10^{-15}$ C/μm is left after the

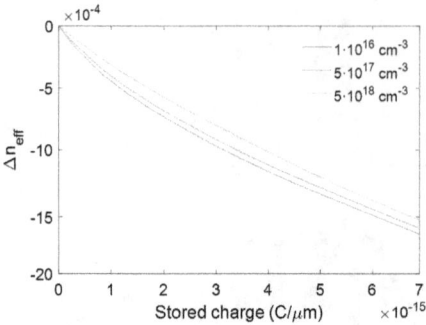

Figure 3.4: Effective index change as a function of the stored charge for different gate and slab doping concentrations. The same doping has been considered for the gate and the slab

erasing process is completed, although it will not significantly affect the device performance. On the other hand, optical losses of 11.28 dB/mm and 8.24 dB/mm are obtained at the two non-volatile states after the writing and erasing processes, respectively, which would be accomplished with an energy consumption of 1.25 pJ and 5.7 pJ. In addition, the memory structure is also able to work at multiple intermediate stages by decreasing either the time or the voltage applied to the gate. Finally, the retention characteristics have also been analyzed to ensure the endurance of the stored data. As shown in Fig. 3.5(b), above $1.1 \cdot 10^{-3}$ is ensured over a time period of 10 years. A small variability in the erased state is observed during the retention time due to the partial loss of the residual charge, however, the maximum shift corresponds to an effective index change as small as $6 \cdot 10^{-5}$. On the other hand, a more significant variation happens at the written state. Its potential impact on the device performance will be managed through a careful device design to ensure the stability of the optical signal, as it will be explained in the following section

However, to complete the analysis, it is still necessary to verify that the residual charge is

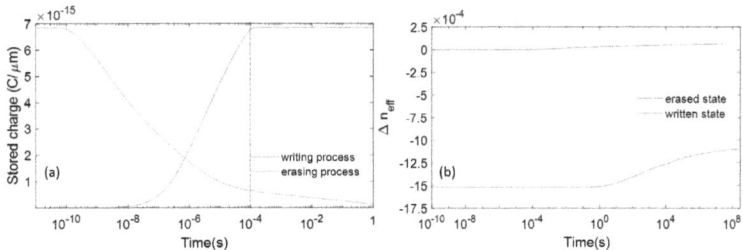

Figure 3.5: (a) Evolution of stored charge with time at the writing and erasing processes and (b) retention characteristics of the effective index variation for 10 years.

not increasingly built up when repetitive cycles are performed. Figure 3.6 shows the charge evolution during three consecutive charge and erase cycles, demonstrating that the value of the trapped charge is stable through time. The reason of this stability is related to the driving forces behind the charging process. The total trapped charge for a certain voltage is driven by the electric field falling through the tunnel oxide. However, this field is determined not only by the applied voltage but also by the charge already trapped inside the trapping layer. Such trapped carriers create an opposite electric field that counteracts to some extent the field created by the applied voltage. The trapping process can keep up while the gate voltage is applied and until the electric field in the tunnel oxide is totally cancelled by that created by the trapped carriers, reaching a saturation value. In our case, the residual charge already present at the end of the erasing process does not affect to the writing process and the same total trapped charge ($7 \cdot 10^{-15}$ C/μm) is achieved for the written state at any cycle.

3.2.2 NON-VOLATILE PHOTONIC DEVICE

A functional non-volatile photonic memory device is achieved by making use of the designed charge trapping waveguide structure. Ring resonators are highly sensitive devices able to

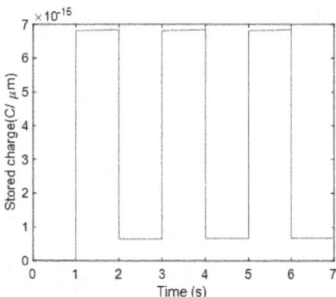

Figure 3.6: Stability of the trapped charge during three consecutive cycles.

transform small index changes to intensity variation in a compact footprint, which makes them the perfect candidate for high density data storage and low energy consumption. Hence, the proposed SAHAS waveguide structure can be embedded in a ring resonator as depicted in Fig. 3.7(a). A ring radius of R=20 μm has been chosen with a gap between the bus waveguide and ring to achieve a power coupling ratio of $|k|=0.15$. In addition, the written state has been chosen to be out-of-the resonance so that the output power is stable during the retention period. Under these conditions, the resonator device will switch between the written and erased points marked in Fig. 3.7(c), which shows the resonances for both states at the beginning and at the end of a retention period of 10 years thus demonstrating how the impact of the charge loss in the optical signal is almost completely mitigated. Furthermore, the output power during the retention time is also depicted in the inset, showing a small variation around 2 dB and extinction ratios above 12 dB during the whole period. Finally, the temporal behavior through repetitive cycles is depicted in Fig. 3.7(d), which is obtained as a result of applying the voltage pattern shown in Fig. 3.7(b). As it can be observed, insertion losses below 1 dB at the written state and extinction ratios of 17 dB are achieved. Furthermore, the photonic memory device is designed to be electrically written but optically read, therefore, the reading process will be only limited by photon lifetime and would enable reading times in the picosecond range, which outperforms current electronic memories and offers ultra-fast access data storage.

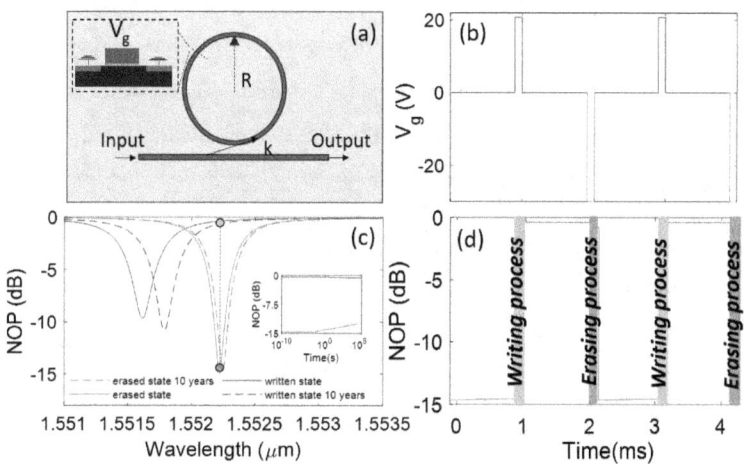

Figure 3.7: (a) Sketch of the non-volatile photonic memory device based on a ring resonator, (b) applied voltage vs. time to change the state of the memory, (c) normalized optical power (NOP) showing photonic resonances at written and erased states and (d) corresponding NOP variation with time at the output port.

Therefore, if we compare with the state-of-the-art of silicon based non-volatile devices presented in Table 3.1, the designed structure shows writing and erasing capabilities in the µs regime, outperforming current solutions in about three orders of magnitude. As opposed to [97] and [40], which are also based in a charge trapping mechanism, the erasure operation is enabled. In addition, retention times over 10 years are at the same time provided. Finally, by embedding the waveguide structure into a ring resonator, extinction ratios above 12 dB and insertion losses well below 1 dB are expected for such device. The characteristics of the proposed device are summarized and compared to the state-of-the-art in Table 3.4.

Technology	V_{write}	V_{erase}	t_{write}	t_{erase}	Ref.
SONOS	10 V	100 V	1 s	2 s	[8]
SONOS	120 V	N/A	~ ms	N/A	[40]
Floating gate	20 V	6 V	600 ms	225 ms	[111,112]
SAHAS	**21.5 V**	**-30 V**	**100 µs**	**100 µs**	**This work**

Table 3.4: Comparison with the state-of-the-art in silicon non-volatile photonic memory devices

4

Towards Pockels effect in strained silicon

THE FIELD OF STRAINED SILICON had a disruptive beginning in 2006, with initial studies claiming to achieve second-order susceptibility values near to those present in commercially available modulators such as LiNbO. However, an increasing number of published studies started to suggest that those values were greatly overestimated. As shown in Chapter 2, carrier effects dominate the DC response of strained Mach-Zehnder interferometers and $\chi^{(2)}$ effects are not measurable in SHG experiments. From the theoretical point of view, published models to date predict much lower second-order susceptibility values for the employed structures. In addition, following studies have highlighted the importance of plasma dispersion effect in the initial findings[7,14,85,109], as well as the low interaction between the optical mode, the electric field and the strain as the other main obstacle hindering Pockels effect[14,109]. The aim of this chapter is, firstly, to present an overview on the theoretical models linking the strain in centrosymmetric materials with the existence of nonlinearities. Secondly, we propose different structures to overcome those obstacles hindering Pockels effect in strained silicon.

4.1 THEORETICAL MODELS ON POCKELS EFFECT IN STRAINED SILICON

The invention of the green laser in 1961 is generally thought to be the origin of the nonlinear field, as it made possible the of light-matter interaction in a new range of optical intensities. The new field emerged rapidly as a consequence of those findings, broadening the limits of optics and giving rise, in the long run, to an enormous number of physical effects fundamental for today optical applications. Nonlinear phenomenon are defined by its nonlinear dependency with the strength of the applied optical field and they cover a variety of processes such as Raman amplification, four-wave mixing, two- and multi- photon absorption, second, third or higher harmonic generation and many others. The development of a theoretical frame is attributed to Bloemberg and Armstrong[46] in the early 80's. Their theory starts by considering the polarization of a material *P(t)*, defined as the dipole moment per unit volume, and its dependency on the applied electric field *E(t)*. The material response to that field can be generalized by expanding the polarization in power series of E(t):

$$P(t) = \epsilon_0 \left[\chi^{(1)} E(t) + \chi^{(2)} E^2(t) + \chi^{(3)} E^3(t) + \ldots \right] \qquad (4.1)$$

The first term in Eq. 4.1 describes the linear response observed at low optical intensities, with the proportionality factor $\chi^{(1)}$ known as the linear susceptibility and being related to the dielectric permittivity as $\varepsilon_r = 1 + \chi^{(1)}$. It is a second order rank tensor, as it can be observed when explicitly writing its components:

$$P_i^{(1)}(\omega, t) = \chi_{ij}^{(1)} E_j(\omega, t) \tag{4.2}$$

The second term, which has a quadratic dependency with the optical intensity, is the responsible of second-harmonic generation (SHG) and Pockels effect (PE). Its proportionality factor is a three-rank tensor and it is known as the second-order susceptibility.

$$P_i^{(2)}(\omega, t) = \chi_{ijk}^{(2)} E_j(\omega, t) E_k(\omega, t) \tag{4.3}$$

To have a more explicit view on the type of processes involved in this phenomena, we can rewrite the previous term as a function of a time varying optical field $E(t) = E_1 e^{i\omega_1 t} + E_1^* e^{-i\omega_1 t} + E_2 e^{i\omega_2 t} + E_2^* e^{-i\omega_2 t}$ involving two frequencies, which results in:

$$P^{(2)}(\omega, t) = \chi^{(2)} \left[E_1^2 e^{2i\omega_1 t} + E_2^2 e^{2i\omega_2 t} + 2E_1 E_2 e^{i(\omega_1 + \omega_2)t} + 2E_1 E_2^* e^{i(\omega_1 - \omega_2)t} + c.c \right] \\ + 2\chi^{(2)} [|E_1|^2 + |E_2|^2] \tag{4.4}$$

The first term describes the processes of SHG for the first and second input frequencies, i.e. the nonlinear polarization depends on two optical fields with a frequency which is two times the originals. The two following terms describe the effects known as sum-frequency generation and difference-frequency generation, and they depend on $(\omega_1 + \omega_2)$ and $(\omega_1 - \omega_2)$, respectively. Finally, the last term represents the appearing of a static electric field because of the material polarization. A phenomenon specially interesting for us appears when an optical field, with frequency $\omega_1 \neq 0$, and an electric field with null frequency $\omega_2 = 0$ or $\omega_1 \gg \omega_2$, are applied at the same time. This process is known as Pockels effect or linear electrooptic effect due to its linear dependency with the applied electric field:

$$P_i^{(2)}(\omega, t) = \chi_{ijk}^{(2)} E_j^{opt.}(\omega_1, t) E_k^{el.}(\omega_2 \ll \omega_1, t) \qquad (4.5)$$

We can proceed with a similar analysis for the third-order susceptibility tensor $\chi^{(3)}$, which gives rise to the third-order polarization responsible of phenomena such as Kerr effect or third harmonic generation (THG):

$$P^{(3)}(\omega, t) = \chi_{ijkl}^{(3)} E_j(\omega, t) E_k(\omega, t) E_l(\omega, t) \qquad (4.6)$$

Expanding the previous definition by considering an incident electric field with three frequencies $E(t) = E_1 e^{i\omega_1 t} + E_1^* e^{i\omega_1 t} + E_2 e^{i\omega_2 t} + E_2^* e^{i\omega_2 t} + E_3 e^{i\omega_3 t} + E_3^* e^{i\omega_3 t}$, we arrive to the following result:

$$P^{(3)}(\omega, t) = 6\chi^{(3)} \sum_{n=1}^{3} \left[E_1 E_1^* + E_2 E_2^* + E_3 E_3^* - \frac{1}{2} E_n E_n^* \right] E_n e^{i\omega_n t}$$
$$+ 6\chi^{(3)} E_1 E_2 E_3 e^{i(\omega_1 + \omega_2 + \omega_3)t} \qquad (4.7)$$
$$+ \chi^{(3)} \sum_{n=1}^{3} E_n^3 e^{3i\omega_n t}$$

$$+6\chi^{(3)} \sum_{i \neq j \neq k}^{3} E_i E_j E_k^* e^{i(\omega_i+\omega_j-\omega_k)t}$$

$$+3\chi^{(3)} \sum_{i \neq j}^{3} E_i^2 E_j e^{i(2\omega_i+\omega_j)t}$$

$$+3\chi^{(3)} \sum_{i \neq j}^{3} E_i^2 E_j^* e^{i(2\omega_i-\omega_j)t} + c.c.$$

The first term of Eq. 4.7 describes a contribution at the same frequency of the incident electric field and causes the material refractive index (both the real and imaginary part) to be dependent on the incident intensity. The second term, also known as third-harmonic generation, happens when three photons at any of the incident frequencies are absorbed and a photon with trice the original frequency (i.e. at the third harmonic) is emitted as a consequence. The rest of the terms are included in the category of four wave mixing, in which three frequencies interact with the nonlinear medium, giving rise to a photon in a fourth frequency which is the result of any combination of the other three.

The n-th order dielectric susceptibility, as defined above, is a macroscopical description of the material ability to polarize in response to an applied electric field. However, when dealing with theories at the atomic level, it is useful to connect the macroscopic definitions with microscopic variables from which its value can be obtained. In fact, it is possible to link the previous susceptibility terms $\chi^{(n)}$ to the energy of the unit cell[9]. On one hand, for a static electric field (or its low frequency limit), the total energy ϵ of a system can be calculated as

$$\epsilon_{total} = -\frac{1}{2}\chi_{ij}^{(1)} E_i E_j - \frac{1}{3}\chi_{ijk}^{(2)} E_i E_j E_k - \frac{1}{4}\chi_{ijkl}^{(3)} E_i E_j E_k E_l + \ldots \qquad (4.8)$$

On the other hand, assuming N independent primitive cells per unit volume, the total energy of the system can be also written as a power expansion of the electric field E:

$$\epsilon_{total} = N\epsilon_{cell} = N\epsilon_{cell}^{(0)} + N\epsilon_{cell}^{(1)} + N\epsilon_{cell}^{(2)} + N\epsilon_{cell}^{(3)} + \ldots \quad (4.9)$$

being $\epsilon_{cell}^{(0)}$ the energy of the system when no electric field is present and the following contributions $\epsilon_{cell}^{(n)}$ dependent on the n-th power of the electric field. By comparing Eqs. 4.8 and 4.9, it is straightforward to identify each term for $\epsilon_{cell}^{(n)}$. This relationship provides us the link between the microscopic and macroscopic descriptions of the energy of a system and allows us to find the static limit of the susceptibility from the expression of ϵ_{total} [57]:

$$\chi_{\alpha_1\alpha_2\ldots\alpha_{r+1}}^{(r)}(0) = -\frac{1}{r!}\frac{\partial^{r+1}\epsilon_{total}}{\partial E_{\alpha_1}\partial E_{\alpha_2}\ldots\partial E_{\alpha_{r+1}}} \quad (4.10)$$

Moreover, Eq. 4.10 is indicating us that to obtain the susceptibility up to the n-th order, it will be necessary to know the expansion of the cell energy up to the n-th +1 order. Finally, focusing on the second-order susceptibility tensor and particularizing to the case of silicon, one can verify that $\chi_{ijk}^{(2)}$ must be identically null.

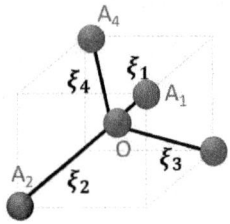

Figure 4.1: Silicon primitive cell showing the bond vectors of each molecular bond. The coordinate system is centred at the central O atom.

This result is the same for any centrosymmetric media and it is a direct consequence of the inversion symmetry of its lattice. The diamond structure of the silicon crystal is depicted in Fig. 4.1. If the same field is applied in one direction and then in the opposite, a centrosymmetric material will respond with an opposite polarization $-P_i^{(2)}(\omega, t)$. However, if we apply this restriction to Eq 4.3 we have:

$$-P_i^{(2)}(\omega,t) = \chi_{ijk}^{(2)}(-E_j(\omega,t))(-E_k(\omega,t)) = \chi_{ijk}^{(2)}E_j(\omega,t)E_k(\omega,t) = P_i^{(2)}(\omega,t) \quad (4.11)$$

But the only way of having $P_i^{(2)}(\omega,t) = -P_i^{(2)}(\omega,t)$ for a non-zero electric field is setting $\chi_{ijk}^{(2)} = 0$. Hence, if we were able to break the centrosymmetry of the material by applying strain, a $\chi_{ijk}^{(2)} \neq 0$ could emerge. In the following subsections, two models linking the strain and the origin of $\chi_{ijk}^{(2)}$ at the atomic level are overviewed. The first one relies in the perturbation theory and the deformation potentials [39,51] while the second is based on the bond orbital model [30].

4.1.1 Deformation potentials

It is possible to derive the expressions for the nonlinear susceptibilities from the time-dependent perturbation theory [77], which describes the interaction of an atomic system under an external excitation (such as an electromagnetic field) at any frequency range. However, simplified and more practical expressions have been obtained relying in the time-independent perturbation theory [57], which treats the optical field as a quasi-static quantity and it is suitable for regimes below the resonant frequency of the material in use. On the other hand, different theories have been developed to describe the effect of strain in the properties of solids. More specifically, deformation potentials have been widely used in the field of electronics to describe the changes induced by strain in the system at equilibrium [62]. They have proven to give accurate results in predicting variables such as the change in semiconductor band structures or the effective electron and hole masses and carrier mobilities [35]. Although optical properties have received less attention until recently, a theoretical model was derived by Govorkov et. al. [39] in 1989 using deformation potentials to predict the SHG present at strained interfaces. This same approach was also successfully used years layer by J. Huang [51] to characterize the stress present at Si(111)-SiO_2 interfaces using Raman spectroscopy. This approach is going to be briefly presented in the following sections.

SECOND-ORDER SUSCEPTIBILITY TENSOR BASED ON PERTURBATION THEORY

In the Schrödinger representation, the dynamics of an atomic system can be specified by the time-dependent wavefunction $\psi(r,t)$ [77]. This wavefunction contains all needed information about the system and it is obtained as the solution of the time-dependent Schrödinger equation:

$$i\hbar \frac{\partial}{\partial t} |\psi(r,t)> = H |\psi(r,t)> \qquad (4.12)$$

In the previous relationship, the "H" represents the Hamiltonian operator, which is obtained as the sum of the kinetic and potential energies of every particle belonging to it:

$$H = H_0 + V(r,t) \qquad (4.13)$$

where V(t) represents any interaction potential of the system with the external environment and H_0 is the Hamiltonian of the free particle. However, for the situation where the optical frequency is lower than the material resonance frequency (usually the case in photonic applications, which work in the free absorption regime) a further simplification can be carried out.

In these conditions, it is possible to approximate the optical field by a quasi-static quantity and apply the time-independent perturbation theory[57]. The starting point of this theory is a general unperturbed and well-known atomic system. The system is therefore described by a known Hamiltonian Ho and a known set of orthonormal eigenstates $|\phi_m>$, which obey the time-independent Schrödinger equation

$$H_0|\phi_m> = E_{0m}|\phi_m> \qquad (4.14)$$

where the Hamiltonian as well as the wavefunctions are now only dependent on spatial variables. Furthermore, the eigenfunctions are taken to be orthonormal to each other and such that Ho is diagonal in this basis. In this representation, E_{0m} will be the known energy values of the unperturbed states. However, when an interaction potential $V(r)$ appears, the initial wavefunctions and energy values are perturbed and become unknown for the new system. To characterize the new system it is necessary, therefore, to obtain the eigenfunctions and eigenvalues of the perturbed Hamiltonian $H = H_0 + \lambda V(r)$, which must obey the time-independent Schrödinger equation

$$H|\Psi_m> = E_m|\Psi_m> \qquad (4.15)$$

where $|\Psi_m>$ are the perturbed eigenstates and E_m their associated energy. In order to solve the system, perturbation theory assumes that the energy E_m and wavefunctions $|\Psi_m>$ of the perturbed system can be expanded into power series of λ:

$$|\Psi_m> = \sum_{n=0}^{\infty} \lambda^n |\psi_m^{(n)}>, \quad E_m = \sum_{n=0}^{\infty} \lambda^n E_m^{(n)} \qquad (4.16)$$

where $E_{0,m} = lim_{\lambda \to 0} E_m$ and $|\phi_m> = lim_{\lambda \to 0} |\Psi_m>$. Considering Eqs. 4.15 and 4.16 and grouping for the same powers of λ, one can obtain the following expressions for the s-th order energy:

$$(H_0 - E_m^{(0)})|\psi_m^{(0)}> = 0 \quad for \ s = 0 \tag{4.17}$$

$$E_m^{(s)} = <\psi_m^{(0)}|V(r)|\psi_m^{(s-1)}> - \sum_{r=1}^{s-1} E_m^{(r)} <\psi_m^{(0)}|\psi_m^{(s-r)}> \quad for \ s > 0 \tag{4.18}$$

where Eq. 4.18 is just the Schrödinger equation for the unperturbed system and $|\psi_m^{(0)}> \equiv |\phi_m>$ and $E_m^{(0)} = E_{0m}$ are, respectively, the wavefunctions and energies of the unperturbed states. As a last step, we just need to define the perturbation potential V(r). The effect of a macroscopic electric field on a pair of bonded atoms is described as a perturbing potential acting on the dipole moment between them:

$$V(r) = e\vec{r}\vec{E} \tag{4.19}$$

with $\vec{r} = x_i \vec{i} + x_j \vec{j} + x_k \vec{k}$ being the bond vector, $r = |\vec{r}|$ the bond length and $\vec{E}$ the electric field. Equation 4.18 gives us the values for the second and third order energies which can be used, together with Eq. 4.10 and Eq. 4.19, to calculate the first and second-order susceptibilities, resulting to be:

$$\chi_{ij}^{(1)} = 2eN \sum_{t \neq m} \frac{<\phi_m|x_i|\phi_t><\phi_t|x_j|\phi_m>}{(E_t - E_m)} \tag{4.20}$$

$$\chi_{ijk}^{(2)} = -3e^2 N \sum_{r \neq m} \sum_{t \neq m} \frac{<\phi_m|x_i|\phi_r><\phi_r|x_j - <\phi_m|x_j|\phi_m>|\phi_t><\phi_t|x_k|\phi_m>}{(E_r - E_m)(E_t - E_m)} \tag{4.21}$$

Finally, if we consider the relationship $\sum_t <\phi_m|L|\phi_t><\phi_t|M|\phi_n> = <\phi_m|LM|\phi_n>$

and replacing $(E_t - E_m)$ and $(E_r - E_m)$ for an average value (the gap energy), we can rewrite the above equations as

$$\chi_{ij}^{(1)} = 2eN \frac{<\phi_m |x_i x_j| \phi_m>}{E_g} \quad (4.22)$$

$$\chi_{ijk}^{(2)} = -\frac{3e <\phi_m|x_i x_j x_k|\phi_m> \chi_{ij}^{(1)}}{2Eg <\phi_m|x_i x_j|\phi_m>} \quad (4.23)$$

where the value of N has been solved from Eq. 4.22 and subsequently used in Eq. 4.23 to replace its value.

The unstrained silicon unit cell

Once we have the general expressions of the susceptibility tensors, we can apply them to our specific problem and check their values for the unstrained case. Electron orbitals in atoms can be classified by their angular momentum. Orbitals with zero, one, two or three units of angular momentum are called the s, p, d, or f orbitals respectively. The silicon atom has fourteen electrons, however, those at the lower energy levels are too localized around its atom to effectively contribute to the covalent bond. Thus, just the four electrons located at the highest energy levels 3s and 3p will be considered to form the bond in the case of Silicon. When two atoms are brought together to form a molecule, the atomic states become combine and, mathematically, they can be expressed as a linear combination of the individual atomic orbitals (LCAO)[44]. The combination of orbitals with lowered energies are called "bonding" orbitals and those with increased energies are called "antibonding" orbitals because they contribute to strengthen the bond or not, respectively. As depicted in Fig. 4.1, the five atoms of the silicon primitive cell are arranged to form four identical covalent bonds with different orientations.

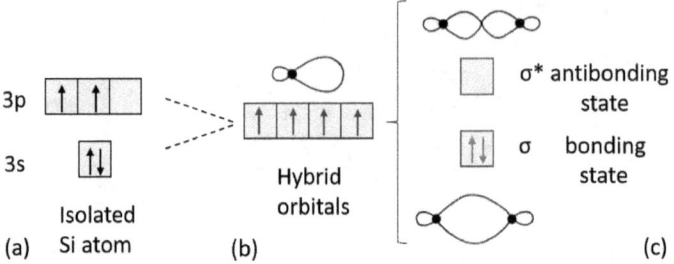

Figure 4.2: (a) Energy levels of the isolated Silicon atom, (b) hybrid orbitals in the silicon unit cell and (c) bonding and antibonding states of the hybrid orbitals.

For each atom, the orbitals of the highest energy level are combined to give rise to a hybrid sp^3 orbital, as shown in Figs. 4.2(a,b), which can be described as a linear combination of the atomic s orbital $|\psi_s>$ and p orbitals $|\psi_p>$:

$$|\psi_O> = \frac{1}{2}|\psi_{s,O}> + \frac{\sqrt{3}}{2}|\psi_{p,O}>, |\psi_A> = \frac{1}{2}|\psi_{s,A}> - \frac{\sqrt{3}}{2}|\psi_{p,A}> \qquad (4.24)$$

where the subscript O denotes the central atom and subscript A any atom in the corners. Using those hybrid orbitals, it is possible to define the bonding and antibonding states, shown in Fig. 4.2(c), for each of the four molecular bonds of the primitive cell:

$$|\psi_1> = \frac{1}{\sqrt{2}}(|\psi_o> + |\psi_A>), |\psi_2> = \frac{1}{\sqrt{2}}(|\psi_o> - |\psi_A>) \qquad (4.25)$$

Both wavefunctions are orthonormal to each other and form a basis of the Hamiltonian H_0, which can be represented in the matrix form as:

$$H_0 = \begin{bmatrix} <\psi_1|H_0|\psi_1> & <\psi_1|H_0|\psi_2> \\ <\psi_2|H_0|\psi_1> & <\psi_2|H_0|\psi_2> \end{bmatrix} = \begin{bmatrix} -\frac{E_g}{2} & 0 \\ 0 & \frac{E_g}{2} \end{bmatrix} \quad (4.26)$$

where E_g is the energy gap, $<\psi_1|H_0|\psi_1> = -\frac{E_g}{2}$ is the energy of the bonding state while $<\psi_2|H_0|\psi_2> = \frac{E_g}{2}$ is the energy of the antibonding state. In this framework, Eq. 4.23 may be written as:

$$\chi^{(2)}_{ijk} = -\frac{3e\chi^{(1)}_{ij}}{2E_g} \sum_{\alpha=1}^{4} \frac{<\psi_1|x_i x_j x_k|\psi_1>}{<\psi_1|x_i x_j|\psi_1>} = -\frac{3e\chi^{(1)}_{ij}}{2E_g} \frac{<\psi_s|r^3|\psi_s>}{<\psi_s|r^2|\psi_s>} \frac{\sum_{=1..4} b_i b_j b_k}{\sum_{=1..4} b_x b_x} \quad (4.27)$$

where x_i, x_j and x_k are the projections on the cartesian axis of each bond vector and each projection can be defined as $x_i = r b_i$ being i=x,y,z. However, the value of $<\psi_s|r^q|\psi_s>$ is null when q is an odd value (see demonstration in Appendix A) and we finally arrive to

$$\chi^{(2)}_{ijk} = 0 \ \ for \ any \ i,j,k \quad (4.28)$$

in agreement with the well-known fact that centrosymmetric crystals do not show nonlinearities of odd order.

STRAINED SILICON AND DEFORMATION POTENTIALS

In our specific problem, the Hamiltonian is perturbed by a term that appears due to the strain and it is proportional to the electron-phonon interaction [39,51]:

$$H = H_0 + H_{e-ph} \quad (4.29)$$

$$H_{e-ph} = \Theta_{mn}\varepsilon_{nm}(R_0 + \xi) = \Theta_{mn}\varepsilon_{nm}(R_0) + \Theta_{mn}\nabla\varepsilon_{nm}\vec{b}^\alpha r = H_D(R_0) + H'_D(\xi) \quad (4.30)$$

where Θ_{mn} is the deformation potential and ε is the strain. We can approximate the strain on the bond $\vec{b}^\alpha$. The Hamiltonian for the perturbed system is now defined as:

$$H = \begin{bmatrix} -\frac{E_g}{2} & <\psi_1|H'_D|\psi_2> \\ <\psi_2|H'_D|\psi_1> & \frac{E_g}{2} \end{bmatrix} = \begin{bmatrix} -\frac{E_g}{2} & S_b \\ S_b & \frac{E_g}{2} \end{bmatrix} \quad (4.31)$$

where S_α takes the value of the off diagonal terms $S_\alpha = <\psi_1|H'_D|\psi_2> = \Theta_{mn}\nabla\varepsilon_{nm}b^\alpha\psi_1|r|\psi_2> = \Theta_{mn}\nabla\varepsilon_{nm}\vec{b}^\alpha <\psi_2|r|\psi_1>$, where we are considering summation over repeated indices.

By diagonalizing the Hamiltonian matrix, it is possible to calculate the eigenvalues and eigenstates of the strained system:

$$E_D = \pm\sqrt{\frac{E_g^2}{4} + S_\alpha^2} \approx \pm\left(\frac{E_g}{2} + \frac{S_\alpha^2}{E_g}\right) \quad (4.32)$$

$$|\psi_1^D> = -f|\psi_1> + g|\psi_2> \quad (4.33)$$

$$|\psi_2^D> = g|\psi_1> + f|\psi_2> \quad (4.34)$$

where the following terms have been defined $\rho = \frac{S_\alpha}{E_g}, g = \frac{1}{\sqrt{1+\rho^2}}$ and $f = \rho g$ and it can be shown that the obtained eigenfunctions are orthogonal to each other. It is important to notice that equations 4.33 and 4.34 relate the wavefunctions of the strained and unstrained crystal, which are known, making the system now solvable. Introducing the previous definitions into Eq. 4.23, the susceptibility of the strained material takes the following form:

$$\chi^{(2)}_{ijk} = -\frac{3e\chi^{(1)}_{ij}}{2E_g} \sum_{\alpha=1}^{4} \frac{<\psi^D_1|x_i x_j x_k|\psi^D_1>}{<\psi^D_1|x_i x_j|\psi^D_1>} = \qquad (4.35)$$

$$= \frac{3e\Theta_{mn}\nabla\varepsilon_{nm}\chi^{(1)}_{ij}}{E_g E_g} \frac{<\psi_s|r^3|\psi_p><\psi_s|r|\psi_p>}{<\psi_p|r^2|\psi_p>} \frac{\sum_{\alpha=1..4} b^\alpha_i b^\alpha_j b^\alpha_k \left(\vec{e}_\nabla \vec{b}\right)}{\sum_{=1..4} b^\alpha_x b^\alpha_x} \qquad (4.36)$$

with $<\psi_s|r^3|\psi_p> = -1.073 \cdot 10^3 (a_B/Z)^3$, $<\psi_p|r^2|\psi_p> = 108 (a_B/Z)^2$ and $<\psi_s|r|\psi_p> = -0.82 (a_B/Z)$ (see detailed calculation in Appendix B).

Finally, let consider a uniaxial deformation with a gradient on the vertical direction y on the same order we observe in our silicon waveguides strained by silicon nitride. Hence, let us assume a strain gradient in the vertical direction $\nabla\varepsilon_{nm} = \frac{\partial \varepsilon_{xx}}{\partial y}\vec{e}_\nabla = \frac{\partial \varepsilon_{xx}}{\partial y}\vec{y}$ with a value of $\frac{\partial \varepsilon_{xx}}{\partial y} \sim 10^4 m^{-1}$. If the cartesian system is the system defined in Fig. 4.1, the four unitary bond vectors of the silicon unit cell would be defined as

$$\vec{b}^1 = \frac{1}{\sqrt{3}}(1,1,1) \quad \vec{b}^2 = \frac{1}{\sqrt{3}}(1,-1,-1) \quad \vec{b}^3 = \frac{1}{\sqrt{3}}(-1,1,-1) \quad \vec{b}^4 = \frac{1}{\sqrt{3}}(-1,-1,1) \quad (4.37)$$

The denominator $\sum_{\alpha=1..4} b^\alpha_x b^\alpha_x$ will be equal to 4/3 and the term $\sum_{=1..4} b^\alpha_i b^\alpha_j b^\alpha_k \left(\vec{e}_\nabla \vec{b}^\alpha\right)$ will take the same value in all non-zero cases. Therefore, the final second order susceptibility tensor takes the following form

$$\chi^{(2)}_{ij} = \begin{bmatrix} 0 & 0 & 0 & 0 & 0 & \chi^{(2)}_{22} \\ \chi^{(2)}_{22} & \chi^{(2)}_{22} & \chi^{(2)}_{22} & 0 & 0 & 0 \\ 0 & 0 & 0 & \chi^{(2)}_{22} & 0 & 0 \end{bmatrix} \qquad (4.38)$$

where contracted notation has been used for j ($1\rightarrow 11, 2\rightarrow 22, 3\rightarrow 33, 4\rightarrow 23, 5\rightarrow 13, 6\rightarrow 12$)

and all non-null terms are equal to

$$\chi_{22}^{(2)} \sim 0.003 pm/V \quad (4.39)$$

and it has been used that $\Theta_u = 10 \, eV, \chi_{11}^{(1)} = 10.8, E_g = 1.1 \, eV, a_B = 52.9 \, pm, Z=4$ [39,51].

4.1.2 BOND ORBITAL MODEL

The bond orbital model was firstly developed by Harrison et. al. in 1975 [43,45] and was used to give accurate prediction for the second-order susceptibility of covalent materials. Very recently, Damas et. al. [30] adapted this model to the case of strained silicon and, the following year, this same model was used to explain the high frequency electro-optic effect demonstrated in a strained silicon Mach Zehnder modulator [12]. The model relays on the concept of the polar energy of a bond between two atoms A and B, which is defined as:

$$\sigma_\varsigma = \frac{<h_\varsigma^A|H|h_\varsigma^A> - <h_\varsigma^B|H|h_\varsigma^B>}{2} \quad (4.40)$$

where h_ς^i are the wavefunctions of the electrons in atom i, being i=A, B. In an unstrained silicon lattice $<h_\varsigma^B|H|h_\varsigma^B> = <h_\varsigma^A|H|h_\varsigma^A>$ and, hence, $\sigma_\varsigma = 0$ indicating that silicon is a non-polar material and, as such, has no second-order nonlinearities.

In a strained silicon lattice, on the other hand, the equation for the polar energy changes to:

$$\sigma_\varsigma = \frac{<h_\varsigma^A|H'|h_\varsigma^A> - <h_\varsigma^{B'}|H'|h_\varsigma^{B'}>}{2} \quad (4.41)$$

where H' is the Hamiltonian of the strained lattice defined as $H' = T + V'_A + V'_B + \sum_{n \neq A,B} V'_n$, and $h_\zeta^{B'}$ the wavefunctions of the electrons in atom B', where B' indicates the new position of atom B after the strain. Because the position of atom A is considered to be the origin of the reference system, its wavefunction h_ζ^A remains unchanged when the strain is applied. The potential $V'_n = V(r - R_n')$ is the crystal potential due to the atom located at R_n'.

With these definitions, it is possible to rewrite both terms in Eq. 4.41 as

$$<h_\zeta^A|H'|h_\zeta^A> = <h_\zeta^A|T+V'_A|h_\zeta^A> + <h_\zeta^A|V'_B|h_\zeta^A> + \sum_{n \neq A,B} <h_\zeta^A|V'_n|h_\zeta^A> \quad (4.42)$$

$$<h_\zeta^{B'}|H'|h_\zeta^{B'}> = <h_\zeta^{B'}|T+V'_B|h_\zeta^{B'}> + <h_\zeta^{B'}|V'_A|h_\zeta^{B'}> + \sum_{n \neq A,B} <h_\zeta^{B'}|V'_n|h_\zeta^{B'}> \quad (4.43)$$

However, the crystal potential can be approximated to $V'_n(r) \sim V_n(r - R_n) - \Delta V_n(r - R_n)$ where $\Delta V_n(r - R_n) = \nabla V_n(r) - R_n u_n$, separating in this way the potential in the unstrained lattice V_n and the contribution of strain V_n. It is important to note that V_n depends only in the parameters of the unstrained system. In addition, the relationship between the wavefunctions of the strained and unstrained crystal must also be considered $h_\zeta^{B'}(r) = h_\zeta^A(R'_B - r)$ together with Eqs. 4.42 and 4.43 in order to express Eq. 4.41 as a function of known parameters:

$$\sigma_\zeta = \frac{<h_\zeta^A|\nabla V_{Ai}|h_\zeta^A>(\vec{u}_B - \vec{u}_{Bi} - \vec{u}_{A_i})}{2} \quad (4.44)$$

where $\vec{u}_B, \vec{u}_{Bi}$ and $\vec{u}_{A_i}$ are the displacements caused by the applied strain to atoms B, B_i and A_i, as depicted in Fig. 4.3.

In addition, those displacements can be calculated by using the strain tensor and taking into account that $\xi_{A_i} = -\xi_{B_i}$, we have:

$$\vec{u}_{Ai} \simeq \bar{\varepsilon}(R_A)\,\xi_{A_i} \tag{4.45}$$

$$\vec{u}_{Bi} \simeq \vec{u}_B + \bar{\varepsilon}(R_B)\,\xi_{B_i} = \vec{u}_B - \bar{\varepsilon}(R_B)\,\xi_{A_i} \tag{4.46}$$

being ξ_{A_i} and ξ_{B_i} the bond vectors of the unstrained unit cell.

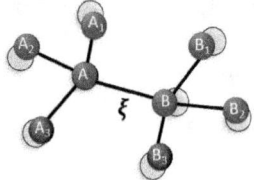

Figure 4.3: The effect of the inhomogeneous strain on the silicon lattice, showing the resultant atom positions after such strain is applied. The bond between atoms A and B is shown together with its first nearest neighbors A_i and B_i. Image adapted from [30].

Finally, a first order Taylor expansion can be made on strain since it changes slowly in distances of the bond length:

$$\varepsilon_{kl}(R_B) = \varepsilon_{kl}(R_A + \xi) \sim \varepsilon_{kl}(R_A) + \nabla \varepsilon_{kl}(R_A)\,\xi \tag{4.47}$$

which allows us to arrive to the final expression for the polarity of the bond ξ:

$$\sigma_\xi = \frac{1}{2}\sum_{i=1}^{3} \theta_i^\xi \Xi(\xi, R)\xi_{A_i} \tag{4.48}$$

where $\Xi = \bar{\bar{\eta}}(R) = \nabla \bar{\varepsilon}(R)$ is the strain gradient tensor and $\theta_i^\xi = <h_\zeta^A|\nabla V_{Ai}|h_\zeta^A>$ is related to the lattice potential on atoms A_i and can be known once the lattice potential V(r) is known. However, θ_i^ξ can be generally expressed as a linear function of two parameters α and β

$$\theta_i^\xi = \alpha\xi + \beta\xi_i \quad (4.49)$$

Thus, once the bond polarity is well defined, it is possible to calculate the dipole moment of a bond. Expanding its value in powers of E up to the second order, it can be approximated to

$$p_\xi^{(2)} \simeq -3\left(\frac{e\gamma}{E_g}\right)^3 \sigma_\xi \cdot (1-S^2)(\xi \cdot E)^2 \xi \quad (4.50)$$

where γ accounts for the distance between the "center of gravity" of each hybrid wavefunction and S is defined as $S = < h_\zeta^A | h_\zeta^{B'} >$. Finally, the macroscopic second-order nonlinear polarization can be obtained as the sum of the dipole moments of the four bonds in the Silicon unit cell divided by its volume v_c

$$P^{(2)} = \frac{1}{v_c}\sum_{\xi=1}^{4} p_\xi^{(2)} = K\sum_{\xi=1}^{4}\sigma_\xi \cdot (\xi \cdot E)^2 \cdot \xi \quad (4.51)$$

where K=$-\frac{3}{v_c}\left(\frac{e\gamma}{E_g}\right)^3(1-S^2) = -1.18 \cdot 10^{29} C^3/m^3 eV^3$.

With these definitions, it is possible to calculate the order of magnitude of the second order susceptibility for the same case as we did with the perturbation theory. In their following work[12], however, Damas et. al. contrast their theoretical model with experimental values and adjust the modeling parameters α and β, achieving a very good agreement with the experimental results. Hence, taking the values $\alpha = -5.1 \cdot 10^{-16}\frac{\varepsilon_0}{Kd^6}$ and $\beta = -24.6 \cdot 10^{-16}\frac{\varepsilon_0}{Kd^6}$ from [12], we can calculate the values of the second-order susceptibility using the bond orbital model. Considering the bond vectors defined in Eq. 4.37 and a consider again a strain gradient of $10^4 m^{-1}$ in the vertical direction, the following susceptibility tensor is obtained:

$$\chi_{ij}^{(2)} = \begin{bmatrix} 0 & 0 & 0 & 0 & 0 & 2\chi^{(2)}_{22} \\ \chi^{(2)}_{22} & \chi^{(2)}_{22} & \chi^{(2)}_{22} & 0 & 0 & 0 \\ 0 & 0 & 0 & 2\chi^{(2)}_{22} & 0 & 0 \end{bmatrix} \quad (4.52)$$

with $\chi^{(2)}_{22} = 2.1 \, pm/V$.

The obtained value is around three orders of magnitude higher than that obtained based on deformation potentials. The origin of such discrepancy has not been explicitly addressed by any published and remains as an open question in the field. Nevertheless, in the work of Hon et. al.[49], it is highlighted that only nearest neighbour interaction is considered in the deformation potentials approach, therefore, ignoring the long-range nature of the Coulomb force. Moreover, as explained in[30], the deformation potentials have been widely used for describing the transport properties of electrons in the energy bands of solids, however, the optical features may not be so precisely predicted in this case because they are related to the properties of electrons localized in the covalent bonds of atoms. In addition, the bond orbital model has been proven to be consistent with experimental results obtained in photonic structures at telecom wavelengths[12]. Therefore, the bond orbital model will be used in the following sections to design an optimized structure where practical values of Pockels effect can be achieved in strained silicon.

4.2 Enhancing Pockels effect in strained silicon waveguides

As shown in previous sections, the values predicted by theoretical models and matched with experimental results point to second order susceptibilities around several pm/V. Such values are not as high as initially thought but represent a starting point from where strained silicon devices can be engineered to enhance Pockels effect and achieve practical values for efficient modulation. On the other hand, we have seen the important role played by free and trapped carriers in strained silicon devices and, in addition, almost a year ago high frequency modulation was demonstrated in a silicon waveguide where a p-i-n junction was used to extract the free carriers from the waveguide core and enhance the weak Kerr effect present in silicon [120]. In this section, the use of a similar p-i-n structure in a strained silicon waveguide is proposed to overcome the issues hindering Pockels effect in strained s ilicon. As a result, effective index change values more than two orders of magnitude higher than those obtained for the undoped structure are predicted.

4.2.1 The index ellipsoid in strained silicon waveguides

Figure 4.4 (a) shows the initial considered structure, consisting on a silicon rib waveguide of 400×220 nm^2 with an etching depth of 140 nm and p-type doping of $10^{15} cm^{-3}$ covered by a silicon nitride layer that acts as a stressor. The cladding thickness has been chosen to be 700 nm with a compressive intrinsic stress of 2 GPa. As depicted in Fig. 4.4(b), the waveguide is rotated around its vertical axis to   the effect of the crystal orientation on the second order susceptibility tensor. The rotation angle, ϕ, is defined with respect to the initial coordinate system, which is aligned with the principal axes of a cubic crystal, i.e. x'= [100], y'= [001], z'= [0-10]. Thus, the four bond vectors of the primitive cell, shown in the inset of Fig. 4.4

(b), must be written as a function of ϕ:

$$\begin{aligned}
\xi_1 &= \frac{d}{\sqrt{3}}\left(\cos\phi + \sin\phi, 1, \sin\phi - \cos\phi\right) \\
\xi_2 &= \frac{d}{\sqrt{3}}(\cos\phi - \sin\phi, -1, \cos\phi + \sin\phi) \\
\xi_3 &= \frac{d}{\sqrt{3}}\left(\sin\phi - \cos\phi, -1, -\cos\phi - \sin\phi\right) \\
\xi_4 &= \frac{d}{\sqrt{3}}(-\cos\phi - \sin\phi, 1, \cos\phi - \sin\phi)
\end{aligned} \qquad (4.53)$$

being d=0.235 nm the length of the unstrained Si-Si bonds. Therefore, the silicon has been considered as an anisotropic material and the variation of the strain with the rotation of the waveguide has also been taken into account[50,125].

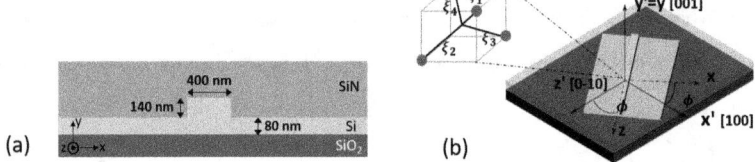

Figure 4.4: (a) Sketch of the strained silicon waveguide covered with a silicon nitride layer of 700 nm and a compressive stress of 2 GPa, and (b) representation of the rotated waveguide showing the reference and waveguide coordinate systems. The reference system is aligned with the crystalline directions of a cubic crystal x'= [100], y'= [001], z'= [0-10]. The four bond vectors of the silicon primitive cell are displayed in the inset

Using Eqs. 4.53 and the bond orbital model described in[30], it is possible to obtain the second order susceptibility tensor as a function of ϕ and the strain gradients inside the waveguide core:

$$\chi^{(2)}_{ij} = \begin{bmatrix} \chi^{(2)}_{11}(\phi) & \chi^{(2)}_{12}(\phi) & \chi^{(2)}_{13}(\phi) & \chi^{(2)}_{14}(\phi) & \chi^{(2)}_{15}(\phi) & \chi^{(2)}_{16}(\phi) \\ \chi^{(2)}_{21}(\phi) & \chi^{(2)}_{22} & \chi^{(2)}_{23}(\phi) & 0 & \chi^{(2)}_{25}(\phi) & \chi^{(2)}_{26}(\phi) \\ \chi^{(2)}_{31}(\phi) & \chi^{(2)}_{32}(\phi) & \chi^{(2)}_{33}(\phi) & \chi^{(2)}_{34}(\phi) & \chi^{(2)}_{35}(\phi) & \chi^{(2)}_{36}(\phi) \end{bmatrix} \quad (4.54)$$

where contracted notation has been used for j ($1 \to 11, 2 \to 22, 3 \to 33, 4 \to 23, 5 \to 13, 6 \to 12$). The explicit form of the tensor coefficients depend on the waveguide rotation angle as:

$$\chi^{(2)}_{11} = \frac{Kd^6}{2 \cdot 27\epsilon_0}[(7\beta - 5\alpha + (3\alpha - \beta)cos(4\phi))\eta_{111} + (9\beta - 3\alpha + \alpha - 3\beta)cos(4\phi)\eta_{221} +$$
$$+ (11\beta - \alpha - (\alpha + 5\beta)cos(4\phi))\eta_{331}]$$

$$\chi^{(2)}_{12} = \frac{Kd^6}{2 \cdot 27\epsilon_0}[(5\beta - 3\alpha + (\alpha + \beta)cos(4\phi))\eta_{111} + 2(3\alpha - \beta)\eta_{221} + (7\beta - \alpha - (\alpha + \beta)cos(4\phi))\eta_{331}]$$

$$\chi^{(2)}_{13} = \frac{Kd^6}{2 \cdot 27\epsilon_0}(3\beta - \alpha)(cos(4\phi) + 1)(\eta_{111} + \eta_{221} + \eta_{331})$$

$$\chi^{(2)}_{15} = \frac{2Kd^6}{27\epsilon_0}cos(2\phi)[(3\beta - \alpha)\eta_{221} + (2\beta - 2\alpha + (\alpha + \beta)cos^2(2))\eta_{111}(4\beta - (\alpha + \beta)cos^2(2\phi)^2)\eta_{331}]$$

$$\chi^{(2)}_{26} = \frac{Kd^6}{27\epsilon_0}[(5\beta - 3\alpha + (\alpha + \beta)cos(4\phi))\eta_{111} + 2(3\beta - \alpha)\eta_{221} + (7\beta - \alpha - (\alpha + \beta)cos(4\phi))\eta_{331}]$$

$$\chi^{(2)}_{21} = \frac{Kd^6}{2 \cdot 27\epsilon_0}[(5\beta - 3\alpha + (\alpha + \beta)cos(4\phi))\eta_{112} + 2(3\beta - \alpha)\eta_{222} + (7 - \alpha - (\alpha + \beta)cos(4\phi))\eta_{332}]$$

$$\chi^{(2)}_{22} = \frac{Kd^6}{27\epsilon_0}(3\beta - \alpha)(\eta_{112} + \eta_{222} + \eta_{332})$$

$$\chi^{(2)}_{23} = \frac{Kd^6}{2 \cdot 27\epsilon_0}[(7\beta - \alpha - (\alpha + \beta)cos(4\phi))\eta_{112} + 2(3\beta - \alpha)\eta_{222} + (5\beta + (\alpha +)cos(4\phi))\eta_{332}]$$

$$\chi_{24} = 0$$

$$\chi^{(2)}_{25} = \frac{2Kd^6}{27\epsilon_0} \cos(2\phi)(3\beta - \alpha)(\eta_{112} + \eta_{222} + \eta_{332})$$

$$\chi^{(2)}_{14} = \frac{Kd^6}{27\epsilon_0} sin(4\phi)(\alpha + \beta)(\eta_{112} - \eta_{332})$$

$$\chi^{(2)}_{16} = \frac{Kd^6}{27\epsilon_0}[(5\beta - 3\alpha + (\alpha + \beta)cos(4\phi))\eta_{112} + 2(3\beta - \alpha)\eta_{222} + (7\beta - \alpha - (\alpha + \beta)cos(4\phi))\eta_{332}]$$
$$(4.55)$$

where $\eta_{111} = \frac{\partial \varepsilon_{xx}}{\partial x}, \eta_{221} = \frac{\partial \varepsilon_{yy}}{\partial x}, \eta_{112} = \frac{\partial \varepsilon_{xx}}{\partial y}, \eta_{222} = \frac{\partial \varepsilon_{yy}}{\partial y}, K = -1.18 \cdot 10^{29} C^3/cm^3 eV^3$, d=0.235 nm the length of the unstrained Si-Si bonds and $\epsilon_0 = 8.85 \cdot 10^{12} Fm^1$ the vacuum permittivity. The effect of both types of gradients are completely decouple, that is, the coefficients are either dependent on the horizontal $(\chi^{(2)}_{11}, \chi^{(2)}_{12}, \chi^{(2)}_{13}, \chi^{(2)}_{15}, \chi^{(2)}_{26})$ or on the vertical strain gradients $(\chi^{(2)}_{21}, \chi^{(2)}_{22}, \chi^{(2)}_{23}, \chi^{(2)}_{25}, \chi^{(2)}_{16}, \chi^{(2)}_{14})$ but never dependent on both.

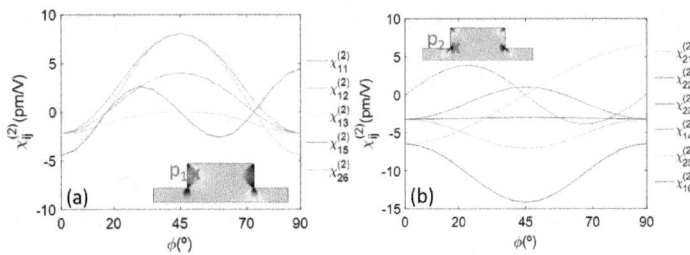

Figure 4.5: Rotational dependency of the susceptibility coefficients dependent on (a) the horizontal and (b) vertical strain gradients taken at p1 and p2, respectively. The insets show the η_{111} and η_{112} strain gradients as well as the chosen points p_1 and p_2, respectively.

To have an idea about the magnitude of the obtained coefficients and how they vary with the rotation of the waveguide, they have been represented in Fig. 4.5 (a) and 4.5 (b). The coefficients shown in Fig. 4.5(a) depend only in η_{ij1}. Their values have been taken at a point where η_{ij1} are maximum. The chosen point, p1(-0.16,0.14) μm, and the η_{111} strain gradient are shown in the inset of Fig. 4.5(a). Analogously, the coefficients shown in Fig. 4.5(b) depend only on η_{ij2} and their values have been taken at point p2 (-0.16,0.07) μm, where the vertical strain gradients are highest. This can be confirmed in the inset of Fig. 4.5(b), where η_{112} and p2 are depicted. It is important to highlight that all of them are in the same order of magnitude and vary between negligible values at the waveguide center up to several pm/V near the waveguide walls, where the strain is higher. Once we know the susceptibility tensor, the index ellipsoid can be calculated by using its general formula [12]:

$$(\eta_{ij} + \Delta\eta_{ij})x_i x_j = 1 \qquad (4.56)$$

being x_i=x, y or z for i=1,2 or 3, respectively, and analogously for x_j, $\eta_{ij} = \epsilon_0^{-1}$ the impermeability tensor of unstrained silicon and $\Delta\eta_{ij}$ the perturbation induced by the Pockels effect, which is given by

$$\begin{bmatrix} \Delta\eta_{xx} \\ \Delta\eta_{yy} \\ \Delta\eta_{zz} \\ \Delta\eta_{yz} \\ \Delta\eta_{xz} \\ \Delta\eta_{xy} \end{bmatrix} = \begin{bmatrix} r_{11} & r_{12} & r_{13} \\ r_{21} & r_{22} & r_{23} \\ r_{31} & r_{32} & r_{33} \\ r_{41} & 0 & r_{43} \\ r_{51} & r_{52} & r_{53} \\ r_{61} & r_{62} & r_{63} \end{bmatrix} \cdot \begin{bmatrix} E_x \\ E_y \\ E_z \end{bmatrix} \qquad (4.57)$$

The applied electric field along the propagation direction E_z has been assumed to be zero and the Pockels coefficients r_{ij} have been obtained from the susceptibility tensor by using the relationship $r_{ij} = -\frac{2}{n_0^4}\chi_{ji}^{(2)}$ [129], with n_0=3.454 the index of unstrained silicon. The resultant index ellipsoid has, in general, non-negligible values for all terms:

$$(\frac{1}{n_0^2}+r_{11}E_x + r_{12}E_y)x^2 + (\frac{1}{n_0^2} + r_{21}E_x + r_{22}E_y)y^2 + (\frac{1}{n_0^2} + r_{31}E_x + r_{32}E_y)z^2 + \\ + 2r_{41}E_x yz + 2(r_{51}E_x + r_{52}E_y)xz + 2(r_{61}E_x + r_{62}E_y)xy = 1 \qquad (4.58)$$

Although we cannot diagonalize the index ellipsoid without disregarding any term, it is possible to extract the explicit form of the refractive index matrix by knowing that[129]

$$\eta_{ij} + \Delta\eta_{ij} = \epsilon^{-1} = (n \cdot n)^{-1} \qquad (4.59)$$

where n is the refractive index matrix in the waveguide coordinate system. Furthermore, we can define the index change due to Pockels effect for a given applied voltage as $\Delta n_{ij}^V = \Delta n_{ij}^V \neq 0 - \Delta n_{ij}^V = 0$:

$$\begin{aligned}
\Delta n_{xx}^V &\approx -\frac{1}{2}n_0^3(r_{11}E_x + r_{12}E_y) \\
\Delta n_{yy}^V &\approx -\frac{1}{2}n_{n0}^3(r_{21}E_x + r_{22}E_y) \\
\Delta n_{zz}^V &\approx -\frac{1}{2}n_{n0}^3(r_{31}E_x + r_{32}E_y) \\
\Delta n_{yz}^V &\approx -\frac{1}{2}n_{n0}^2 r_{41}E_x \\
\Delta n_{xz}^V &\approx -\frac{1}{2}n_{n0}^2(r_{51}E_x + r_{52}E_y) \\
\Delta n_{xy}^V &\approx -\frac{1}{2}n_{n0}^2(r_{61}E_x + r_{62}E_y)
\end{aligned} \qquad (4.60)$$

As it is possible to see from Eqs. 4.60, the effective index change is directly proportional to the Pockels coefficients and the applied electric field, therefore, it should be possible to find an optimum waveguide orientation and electrode configuration that maximize the index change.

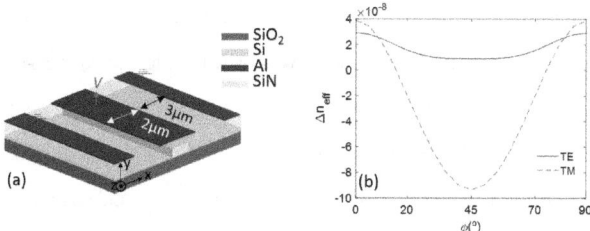

Figure 4.6: (a) Sketch of the electrode configuration used to the strain induced electro-optic effect and the corresponding effective index change for (b)TE (blue) and TM (red) modes as a function of φ for an applied voltage of -15 V. Results are obtained either by considering all refractive index elements (solid lines) or only diagonal elements (dashed lines)

We will start first by studying the electrode configuration used in most experimental works on strained silicon[7,13,15,29,30,75,92], which is depicted in Fig. 4.6(a). The voltage is applied in the central electrode while the laterals are electrically grounded. The space and width of the electrodes have been optimized to 3 μm and 2 μm, respectively, to reach maximum effective index variation. By using Eqs. 4.60, the effective index change as a function of φ has been obtained at the working wavelength (λ=1.55 μm) by using a FEM based software (COMSOL). The result is depicted in Fig. 4.6(b) for TE and TM modes and an applied voltage of -15 V. All refractive index elements were considered at first and have been depicted with solid lines in Fig. 4.6(b). However, crossed terms play in general a secondary role in the effective index change value, as it is revealed by the calculation made without considering those terms and depicted with dashed lines. A remarkable variation with φ is predicted specially for the TM mode, varying between negative and positive values. In fact, a null effective index change is predicted for 25° and 65° and reaches a highest negative value of $-9 \cdot 10^{-8}$ at 45°. This variation with φ is related not only to the change in the refractive index but also due to the variation of its distribution inside the waveguide core and, therefore, in the overlap with the optical mode. To show this more clearly, the index change of the Δn_{yy}^V element (which is specially influent in the TM mode) is depicted in Fig. 4.7(a) at $\phi=0°$ (top) and $\phi=45°$ (bottom) for an applied voltage of -15 V. A quite strong change from positive to negative values can be observed near the waveguide walls between both situations, change that is then reflected in the variation of the effective index when the waveguide is rotated.

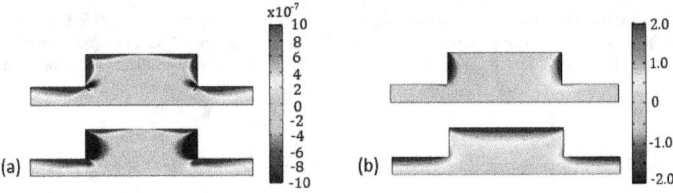

Figure 4.7: (a) Contour plot of n_{yy}^V at $\phi=0°$ (top) and $\phi=45°$ (bottom) for an applied voltage of -15 V and (b) contour plot of the E_x (top) and E_y (bottom) DC electric field components (V/μm).

On the other hand, both TE and TM modes reach the highest positive values of $3 \cdot 10^{-8}$ and $4 \cdot 10^{-8}$, respectively, at 0°, which is still very low in comparison with that obtained by the plasma dispersion effect. The explanation of these low results can be attributed to different origins. First, there is an intrinsic limitation due to the small Pockels coefficients we are considering. The values of the modelling parameters have been taken from [12], where experimental results were used to extract such values. In addition, there is an attenuation of the Δn_{yy}^V due to the location of both, the electric field and the strain gradients at the waveguide borders, areas with little interaction with the optical mode. The first effect is well captured in Fig. 4.7(b), where the electric field inside the waveguide core is depicted. The electric field is quite strong at the waveguide borders. However, it is screened due to the carrier accumulation at the Si-SiN interface and rapidly decreases to almost negligible values at the waveguide center. We can observe the same trend in Fig. 4.7(a), where the change in the refractive index elements is strong near the Si-SiN interfaces but decreases several orders of magnitude when approaching the waveguide core. Finally, the effective index change due to plasma dispersion effect has also been simulated, obtaining values around $1.4 \cdot 10^{-5}$ for an applied voltage of -15 V, i.e. three orders of magnitude higher than those predicted for the strain induced Pockels effect and, thus, completely masking it in static measurements.

4.2.2 The effect of a p-i-n junction

As it has been briefly discussed before, the screening of the electric field is one of the main factors limiting the strength of Pockels effect. In this second section, the use of a p-i-n junction is going to be studied to overcome this problem. To do so, highly doped regions are placed at both sides of the waveguide core with an opposite dopant concentration of $10^{20} cm^{-3}$. The distance from the waveguide center is chosen to be 400 nm to avoid high absorption losses due to the interaction between the optical field and the highly doped areas. We will begin by studying the behavior of the p-i-n junction with the same electrode configuration as that used in the undoped case, depicted in the top image of Fig. 4.8(a). In this case, for low values of the applied reverse bias, the junction keeps the free carriers outside the waveguide core and avoids their masking effect. However, for higher applied voltages, the external electric field becomes stronger than the built-in electric field of the junction. In this situation, the external field easily moves the carriers from the highly doped regions to the waveguide core, therefore, cancelling the beneficial effect of the p-i-n structure. In order to avoid this scenario, lateral electrodes have been designed to be in contact with the p^{++} and n^{++} areas, as depicted in the top image of Fig. 4.8(b). Therefore, the external voltage will be applied not only on the central but also on the lateral electrode contacting the p^{++} region. In this way, the horizontal field created by the p-i-n junction will be strengthened with the applied voltage and will keep the free carriers away from the core. On the other hand, the central electrode will be mainly in charge of enhancing the vertical electric field.

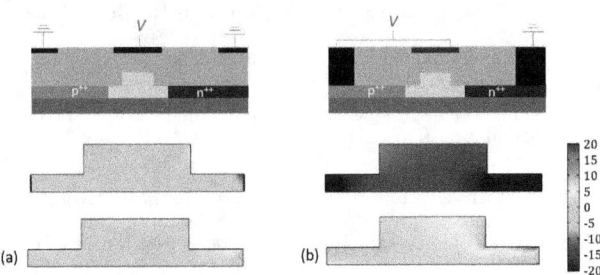

Figure 4.8: (a) Sketch of the configuration 1 (top) and contour plot of the Ex (middle) and E_y (bottom) components of the electric field inside the waveguide core (V/μm) for an applied voltage of -15 V. (b) Sketch of the configuration 2 (top) and contour plot of the Ex (middle) and E_y (bottom) electric fields inside the waveguide core for this configuration for an applied voltage of -15 V.

Figure 4.8 the E_x (middle images) and E_y (bottom images) components of the electric field inside the waveguide core for the p-i-n junction with top and top plus lateral electrodes, respectively, which will be referred to in the following as "configuration 1" and "configuration 2". A strong improvement is clearly observed for the latter configuration, in which both Ex and Ey components of the electric field reach values of several and even tens Volts per micron at the waveguide center, while in the first situation the field does not reach 1 V/μm.

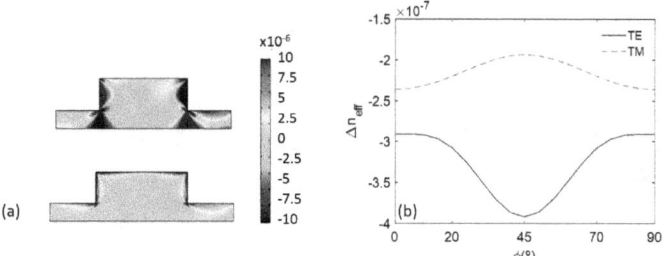

Figure 4.9: (a) Contour plot of n_{yy}^V for the configuration 1 (bottom) and configuration 2 (top) at ϕ=0° for an applied voltage of -15 V and (b) corresponding effective index change for TE and TM modes.

Thanks to the electric field enhancement, the refractive index change values are improved by around two orders of magnitude with respect to those obtained with the standard configuration. This can be observed in Fig. 4.9(a), which shows the index change of the Δn_{yy}^V element for the configuration 1 (bottom) and configuration 2 (top) at ϕ=0° for an applied voltage of -15 V. However, the resulting effective index change is a complex combination of the overlap between optical fields and Δn_{yy}^V, which results in a lower effective index change. As observed in Fig. 4.9(b), the best results are obtained at ϕ=0° for TM and at 45° for TE with values of $-2.3 \cdot 10^{-7}$ and $-3.9 \cdot 10^{-7}$, respectively. This implies an improvement of a factor of 7.6 and 4.3 for TE and TM modes with respect to the best cases of the initial structure. At the same time, the effective index change due to plasma dispersion effect decreases to around 10^{-5}, which is 7.4 times smaller with respect to the initial case.

4.2.3 THE EFFECT OF AN ASYMMETRIC CLADDING

Although high values around 10^{-5} are observed in some areas of Fig. 5.8(a) for the configuration 2, the low interaction with the optical mode and the overlapping with areas of opposite Δn_{yy}^V gives a resulting effective index change of around 10^{-7}, i.e. two orders of magnitude weaker. In order to improve this situation, the use of an asymmetric cladding is analyzed in this section. A scheme of the structure is depicted in Fig. 4.10(a). Half of the waveguide is covered by a silicon nitride cladding with a high compressive stress of 2 GPa while the other half is covered by a silicon nitride with a tensile stress of 1.25 GPa. Both chosen values are feasible and already experimentally demonstrated in different published works[28,120]. Figure 4.10(b) shows the contour plot of the Δn_{yy}^V element of the refractive index matrix. Thanks to the asymmetry in the applied deformation, a high strain is located at the waveguide center. In addition, most of the waveguide core has an index change of the same sign, which results in a remarkable improvement of the overlap with the optical mode.

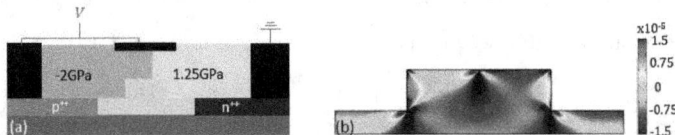

Figure 4.10: (a) Sketch of the proposed structure with the left half of the cladding with a compressive stress of 2 GPa (light blue) and the right half with a tensile stress of 1.25 GPa (violet) and (b) contour plot of the n_{yy}^V refractive index element for φ=0° and an applied voltage of -15 V.

In this case, the maximum effective index change increased up to $-6 \cdot 10^{-6}$ for TE at a rotation angle of ϕ=0°, as shown in Fig. 4.11. Such result represents an increase of more than two orders of magnitude with respect to the initial configuration. Furthermore, a noticeable result is also obtained for the TM mode, with a maximum effective index change of $-3 \cdot 10^{-6}$

also for $\phi=0°$. Finally, the plasma dispersion effect is not affected by the stress of the cover layer and, therefore, still has a value of around 10^{-5}.

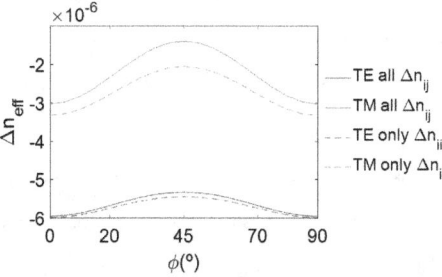

Figure 4.11: Effective index change for TE and TM modes as a function of φ for an applied voltage of -15 V. Results are obtained either by considering all refractive index elements (solid lines) or only diagonal elements (dashed lines).

Therefore, the proposed methods address the underlying causes hindering Pockels effect in strained silicon and offer an improvement of the effective index change of a factor of 200 with respect to the conventional structure considered until now. The p-i-n junction is used to keep the carriers away from the waveguide core and enhance, in this manner, the applied electric field. The asymmetric cladding is used to strongly increase the overlap between the strain and the optical mode, preventing areas of opposite sign to counteract each other. Such improvements lead to a significant step forward in the performance of strained silicon devices, and, in addition, they could help to unambiguously demonstrate Pockels effect as the cause of the measured electro-optic response.

4.3 A $Si_{1-x}Ge_x$ slot approach for the mid-IR range

In the previous section, a significant enhancement of the strain induced Pockels effect has been achieved by including a p-i-n junction and manipulating the stress of the cladding, however, the way of applying such strain (mainly using a stressing silicon nitride cover), has not barely changed since the concept was proposed[7,14,22,28,30,53,85]. This situation contrasts when compared to the microelectronic industry, where a much diverse variety of methods for applying strain can be found, from bridge like structures[81] to lattice mismatched layers[74]. More specifically, the use of silicon-germanium alloys ($Si_{1-x}Ge_x$) to apply strain is a mature technique employed to tune the electrical and optical properties of silicon and other materials. For example, in reverse embedded-SiGe MOSFETs the elastic relaxation of a buried compressive SiGe layer is used to induce tensile strain in the silicon. In this manner, it is possible to enhance, among others, the carrier mobilities in the channel[34]. The SiGe system is also broadly used to engineer structures such as light-emitting diodes[16] or single-electron quantum devices[38]. Moreover, very recently efficient direct-bandgap emission has been achieved in SiGe alloys[33] marking a milestone in the photonics field and making this material system an ideal platform for combining electronic and photonic devices in the same chip.

In this section, a slot structure made of a Ge-SiGe-Si-Ge heterojunction is proposed to increase the strain applied to the silicon layer as well as its interaction with the optical mode and electric field. The structure has been designed to work in the 2 μm region, where the optical losses of Ge are low. In Sec. 4.3.1 the structure is firstly designed and, in Sec. 4.3.2 the achievable effective index change is estimated.

4.3.1 THE GE-SIGE-SI-GE SLOT STRUCTURE

The proposed device consists on a layered structure grown on a (100) silicon SOI wafer. The bottom and top Germanium layers have been chosen to be 200 nm thick. Sandwiched between them, a three layer stack will be epitaxially grown. The main goal is to have a highly stressed silicon film but, in order to do that, a smooth transition is needed between the germanium and silicon because, if the lattice mismatch is too large, dislocations in the interface will appear and no stress will be transferred to the silicon film. Therefore, two SiGe films are epitaxially grown from the Ge bottom layer with x=0.65 and x=0.35 germanium concentrations,respectively. The silicon layer is then grown on top of them. A thickness of 10 nm has been chosen for the three layers taking into account the critical thickness to avoid the formation of misfit dislocations[2]. A fully relaxed 200 nm thick Ge top layer is finally grown on top of the silicon with the aim of having an inhomogenous strain. Moreover, there is no need for the Ge top layer to be in its crystalline state, thefore, an amorphous Ge layer could be grown, if needed, to ease the fabrication process . A sketch of the designed structure is shown in Fig. 4.12.

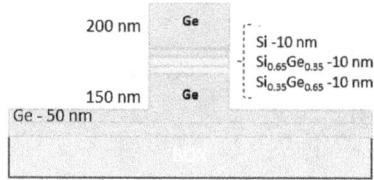

Figure 4.12: The proposed Ge-SiGe-Si-Ge slot structure

STRAIN APPLIED TO THE SILICON LAYER

The strain due to the SiGe layers has been simulated with SILVACO Athena and Atlas software packages[110] and it is dependent on the Ge concentration of each layer. Values near to 10^{-2} for the strain are found inside the three layer stack, as it can be observed in Fig. 4.13 (a), and even higher in the edges due to the effect of the etching process. Such values are around one order of magnitude more intense than those of the silicon-silicon nitride waveguide configuration. Moreover, the strain gradients reach values about 10^5 m^{-1}, as depicted in Fig. 4.13 for the $\frac{\partial \varepsilon_{xx}}{\partial x}$ and $\frac{\partial \varepsilon_{xx}}{\partial y}$ components. But even more interesting is the fact that the vertical $\frac{\partial \varepsilon_{xx}}{\partial y}$ strain gradients in Fig. 4.13 (c) are mainly negative, as opposed to what happens for $\frac{\partial \varepsilon_{xx}}{\partial x}$ in Fig. 4.13 (b). In this case, the horizontal strain gradient shows a completely anti-symmetric distribution, with areas of opposite sign canceling each other out. In fact, this was one of the main issues observed in the silicon-silicon nitride waveguides, as also discussed in Sec. 4.2.2 and depicted in Fig. 2.20 of Chapter 2. The three-layer SiGe stack, therefore, allows to avoid counteracting strain areas, similarly to what happened with the asymmetric stress cladding but with larger strain gradients.

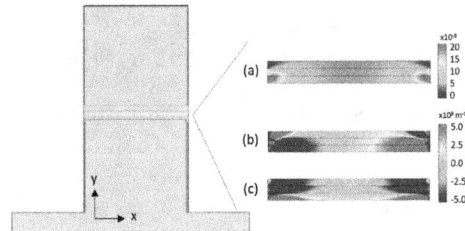

Figure 4.13: Contour plot of the (a) $_{xx}$ strain component and the (b) horizontal $\frac{\partial \varepsilon_{xx}}{\partial x}$ and (c) vertical $\frac{\partial \varepsilon_{xx}}{\partial y}$ strain gradients for ε_{xx} in the silicon layer.

ELECTRIC FIELD STRENGTH INSIDE THE STRAINED SILICON LAYER

To simulate the electrical behavior of the device, the correct values for the $Si_{1-x}Ge_x$ alloys must be considered. Most of optical and electrical parameters follow a linear relationship with concentration, which is the case of the band gap and dielectric constant[65]. Therefore, they have been obtained by interpolating from pure Si and Ge values. Table 4.1 summarizes the parameters used in the simulations.

	parameter	units	value
Silicon	Refractive index		3.451
	Band Gap	eV	1.12
	Electron affinity	eV	4.05
	Dielectric constant		11.9
$Si_{0.35}Ge_{0.65}$	Refractive index		3.875
	Band Gap	eV	0.851
	Electron affinity	eV	4.018
	Dielectric constant		14.57
$Si_{0.65}Ge_{0.35}$	Refractive index		3.680
	Band Gap	eV	0.959
	Electron affinity	eV	4.032
	Dielectric constant		13.34
Ge	Refractive index		4.216
	Band Gap	eV	0.66
	Electron affinity	eV	4.0
	Dielectric constant		16.0

Table 4.1: Si, Ge and $Si_{1-x}Ge_x$ material parameters at 2 μm.

To obtain the results, the voltage (Vg) has been applied to the top Ge layer while the bottom one has been grounded. The resulting electric field in the whole structure for an applied voltage of 12V is shown in Fig. 4.14(a) with the (b) horizontal and (c) vertical components inside the three layer stack. Moreover, Fig. 4.14(d) shows also E_y along the vertical line marked in Fig. 4.14(a) to show the electric field values inside the structure. In fact, the maximum voltage that can be applied to the device is limited at 12 V and -5 V at positive and negative voltages, respectively, by the breakdown field of germanium (12.5 V/μm)[72]. This value is also marked in Fig. 4.14(d) as indication. It is possible to observe in the images of Fig. 4.14 how the heterojunction helps to concentrate the electric field inside the silicon. While a gradual rise on the electric field values can be observed in Ge, a steep increase happens at the Si and SiGe layers, reaching maximum electric fields of around ± 17 V/μm in the silicon film. Hence, the higher electric field intensity located in the strained silicon layer will further contribute to enhance Pockels effect. In addition, it is important to notice the asymmetric behavior between positive and negative voltages, obtaining higher electric fields for negative applied biases and, therefore, reaching the limit due to the germanium breakdown field at lower values. This behavior will also be reflected in the relationship between refractive index change and applied voltage, as we will see in the following.

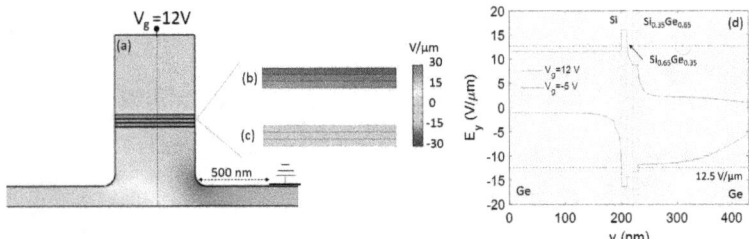

Figure 4.14: (a) Electric field norm for the whole structure and (b) E_x and (c) E_y components in the strained Si-Ge stack at 12 V. (d) Values of the E_y component along the vertical line depicted in (a) for 12 V and -5 V.

4.3.2 THE STRAIN INDUCED EFFECTIVE INDEX CHANGE

Thanks to the smaller refractive index of Si and SiGe films compared to that of germanium, the guided optical mode is mainly concentrated in the strained stack, as it is shown in Fig. 4.15 (a). The simulation has been carried out at 2 μm to avoid high optical losses coming from the germanium layers. The refractive index change of silicon has been calculated for an applied voltage of 12V taking into account the bond orbital model[30], where the same values for the experimental parameters α and β determined in[28] at 1.55 μm have been considered as an approximation. The results for the Δn_{yy} are depicted in Figure 4.15 (b), where values even larger than 10^{-4} can be observed. However, germanium is also a centrosymmetric material which lacks $\chi^{(2)}$ non-linearities due to the inversion symmetry of its lattice. The highly strained SiGe layers, therefore, could also contribute in a similar way as silicon to the final effective index change. Furthermore, the effect of those layers should be analyzed in order to know how they can affect the device performance. Hence, the refractive index for the SiGe films has also been calculated, approximating the same α and β values as those for silicon. In addition, a value of 0.5 has been used for the S parameter, related to the overlap between hybrid orbitals. The values for the bond length and γ have been interpolated considering those of pure silicon (d=0.235 nm, γ=1.4[30]) and germanium (d=0.245 nm, γ=1.6[44]). The Δn_{yy} for the three layers is depicted in Fig. 4.15 (c).

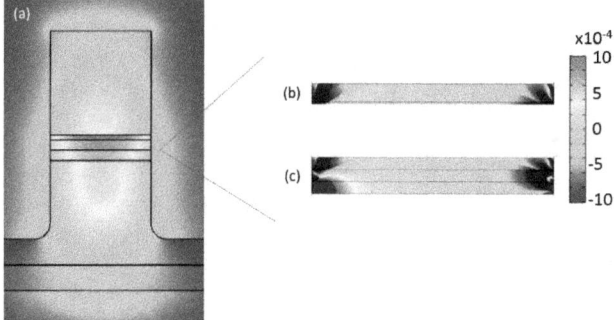

Figure 4.15: (a) Optical mode and n_{yy} refractive index change for (b) silicon and (c) the three layer Si-SiGe stack.

Then, the effective index change of the optical mode has been calculated considering two scenarios: one in which only the silicon film contributes to the final effective index change and another in which the three layers are considered. The results are shown in Fig. 4.16, where it is possible to see that the best outcomes are obtained when the Si plus the two SiGe layers are taken into account. A smaller effective index change is obtained when only silicon is considered, in which case a total value of $\sim 3 \cdot 10^{-5}$ is obtained when a sweep between -5 V and 12 V is performed. Again, an asymmetric behavior for positive and negative voltages is observed for the effective index change as a consequence of the asymmetry in the electric field already described in the previous section. On the other hand, more encouraging outcomes are obtained when the three layers are considered. In this case, a total index change of $\sim 7 \cdot 10^{-5}$ is achieved. This result improves in more than three orders of magnitude the expected results for the usual silicon-silicon nitride structure and by around 12 times the results obtained in Sec. 4.2.

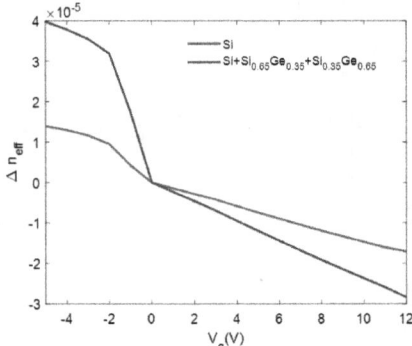

Figure 4.16: Effective index change as a function of the applied voltage considering the contribution of silicon (blue) and silicon plus both SiGe layers (red).

Moreover, such values would hugely facilitate the experimental demonstration of Pockels effect in strained silicon and, if proven, could mark a milestone in the silicon photonics fiels. Hence, the Pockels effect could be exploited with the discussed structure in which almost practical values for Pockels coefficients could be achieved. The proposed device has been designed to work at the beginning of the mid-IR range, at around 2 μm, however, whenever experimental values for the α and β parameters of the bond orbital model are available at higher wavelengths, the same design could be replicated at higher wavelengths in the mid-IR range. Therefore, the silicon-germanium system allows to efficiently strain the silicon layer possibiliting, at the same time, a high electric and optical field overlap. In addition, the Si/SiGe material system is a mature technology currently used in the microelectronic industry to induce strain, thus, offering a CMOS compatible route for implementing efficient silicon modulation.

5

Conclusions

5.1 CONCLUSIONS AND FUTURE WORK

The main goal of this was to employ the strained silicon technology to enable an efficient Pockels effect. Such functionality has been only achieved in silicon by integrating other materials such as $LiNbO_3$ or $BaTiO_3$, however, this approach strongly limits the integration with the electronic platform. In this context, strained silicon would offer a new route for enabling highly efficient modulation in a low cost and fully CMOS compatible manner. Chapter 1 was dedicated to give a clear description of how strained silicon fits within the photonics picture as well as to present the possibilities and challenges of this technology.

On the other hand, Chapter 2 aimed at further investigating how free and trapped carriers were impacting the electro-optic response of strained silicon devices. The dependence on crystal orientation as well as the influence of stress magnitude and stress type were analyzed in strained Mach-Zehnder interferometers by means of silicon nitride layers with different intrinsic stress. Unfortunately, no correlation between the electro-optic response and the magnitude of strain was found. By contrary, the measured data revealed the strong influence of free carriers and how the variations of the silicon nitride trapped carrier concentrations were behind the linear response between effective index change and voltage, many times used to attribute the obtained results to Pockels effect. Furthermore, the annealing experiments also revealed no correlation between applied strain and maximum effective index change and Raman measurements supported the hypothesis that trapped and free carriers were the main mechanisms behind the obtained results. Finally, second-harmonic generation experiments performed in silicon waveguides with different crystal orientations also revealed the absence of a measurable strain induced $\chi^{(2)}$. Hence, all the experimental data reinforced the hypothesis of a rather weak Pockels effect.

Despite those findings, the carrier trapping effects observed in the fabricated devices were the seed for the work developed in Chapter 3, where a solution for a CMOS compatible non-volatile electro-optic memory was proposed. The non-volatile memory functionality is another building block still lacking in silicon. Several approaches have been proposed to date based on the concept of the flash electronic memory. Among them, those based on a floating gate approach show some limitations coming from the complexity of the device and from the chosen technology, which causes the discharge of the device whenever there is a defect on the thin tunnel oxide. On the other hand, those based on a charge trapping scheme show no erasing capabilities or, if they do, they need voltages above 100 V. Our proposed device, however, works by making the polysilicon gate part of the optical guiding structure. In this manner, it is possible to reduce the blocking oxide, thus, enabling the erasing process and leading to writing and erasing capabilities in the microsecond range with voltages between 20 V and 30 V. Such features outperform the current state-of-the-art of silicon based photonic memories following a similar approach.

Finally, in Chapter 4, an overview of the theoretical models on strain induced $\chi^{(2)}$ were presented. The discrepancies shown between those models in the values of $\chi^{(2)}$ were briefly discussed, however, it is important to highlight that a more thorough explanation remains as a question to be addressed. After that, two approaches were presented to tackle the main limiting factors hindering Pockels effect: a p-i-n junction with an asymmetric stress cladding and a Si-Ge slot waveguide. In the first case, the p-i-n junction acts by suppressing the masking effect of the free carriers and enhances the electric field inside the waveguide core. In addition, to improve the overlap between the strain and the optical mode, an asymmetric cladding was proposed. This solution made possible to apply the strain in the waveguide center and to avoid counteracting areas with opposite refractive index changes. As a result, a total effective index change of around $\sim -6 \cdot 10^{-6}$ was reached, improving in a factor of 200 the results of the conventional silicon-silicon nitride waveguide structure used up to date. Concerning this result, the influence of Kerr effect has also been recently proven in p-i-n junctions[18,120]. Therefore, its interplay with Pockels effect in the proposed structure should be analyzed and remains as a future work. On the other hand, regarding the SiGe proposed structure, a Si-$Si_{0.65}Ge_{0.35}$-$Si_{0.35}Ge_{0.65}$ stack was used to improve the strain applied in the silicon. Strain gradients around one order of magnitude higher than those obtained with the previous approach, together with a highly concentrated optic field made possible to achieve effective index change values near to 10^{-4}. This result represents an improvement in more than three orders of magnitude with respect to the commonly used silicon-silicon nitride structure. The experimental proof of those values would be the following step. Such experimental demonstration would further validate the obtained results and could have a huge impact in the field.

The proposed structures, therefore, make possible a considerable enhancement of strain induced Pockels effect, however, the resultant effective index change is still rather low for allowing a practical modulation. Other ways of applying strain, for instance, using piezoelectric materials could be also explored. Such approach has the advantage of allowing to dynamically change the strain and, perhaps, to find an optimum way of applying it. Additional strategies to further enhance the electro-optical modulation performance would also be useful. The combination of the proposed p-i-n structure with a photonic crystal to strength the interaction of the optical mode with the strained areas, as demonstrated in the seminal work of Jacobsen[54], could be a promising option in this line.

www.ingramcontent.com/pod-product-compliance
Lightning Source LLC
LaVergne TN
LVHW012000070526
838202LV00054B/4981